ARTISANAL COCKTAILS

ARTISANAL COCKTAILS

Drinks Inspired by the Seasons
from the Bar at Cyrus

SCOTT BEATTIE

Photography by **Sara Remington**

TEN SPEED PRESS
Berkeley | Toronto

Ten Speed Press
PO Box 7123
Berkeley, California 94707
www.tenspeed.com

Distributed in Australia by Simon and Schuster Australia, in Canada by Ten Speed Press
Canada, in New Zealand by Southern Publishers Group, in South Africa by Real Books, and
in the United Kingdom and Europe by Publishers Group UK.

Jacket and text design by Toni Tajima
Prop styling by Nissa Quanstrom and Peggi Jeung
Photography assistance by Adi Nevo

Library of Congress Cataloging-in-Publication Data
Beattie, Scott, bartender.
    Artisanal cocktails : drinks inspired by the seasons from the bar at Cyrus / Scott Beattie ;
photography by Sara Remington.
       p. cm.
    Includes index.
    Summary: "A full-color collection of fifty cocktail recipes using organic, sustainable pro-
duce, handcrafted ingredients, and local artisanal spirits, from the bar manager at the award-
winning Cyrus Restaurant"—Provided by publisher.
    ISBN-13: 978-1-58008-921-0
    ISBN-10: 1-58008-921-6
1. Cocktails. 2. Cyrus Restaurant. I. Title.
TX951.B335 2008
641.8'74—dc22

                              2008013997

Printed in China
First printing, 2008

1 2 3 4 5 6 7 8 9 10 — 12 11 10 09 08

CONTENTS

Acknowledgments   viii

Introduction:

    Drinks Inspired by the Seasons   x

WINTER   9

Hello Cello   12

Meyer Beautiful (My, You're Beautiful)   13

Pelo del Perro (Hair of the Dog)   15

Waverly Place Echo   17

Lotus Potion   23

Bleeding Orange   26

Thai Monkey   33

Hot Indian Date   35

Caipirinha   37

Classic Margarita   41

Beachfire Margarita   42

Flores Margarita   43

THE IMPORTANCE OF PROPER JUICING   10

SPICED SIMPLE SYRUPS   20

FOAMS   28

SALTED AND SUGARED RIMS   38

SPRING   45

April Shower   47

Frondsong   49

Gin Kimchi   51

Cuba Libre   55

Gin and Tonic   57

Dark and Stormy   59

Mariposa Aviation   62

Rudd Negroni   63

Frankfort Manhattan   65

Mendo Side Car   67

Handy Sazerac   69

Pappy Old-Fashioned   70

The Last Word   71

Bourbon Infused with Vanilla and

    Citrus Peel   72

Rhubarbarella   75

Beau Regards   76

SPRING GIN COCKTAILS   46

ULTIMATE PICKLING LIQUID   52

PERFECT ICE CUBES   58

SODAS AND MIXERS   60

STAINING   73

SUMMER   79

Thai Boxer   81
Sunny and Dry   83
Mint Julep   85
Mojito   86
Blackberry Lick   89
Huck Yu   91
Fraser River Sour   92
Westside Bellini   95
Plum Dandy   99
Celery Mary   103
The Upstairs Neighbor   105
Creole Watermelon   107
Pimm's Cup   109

WHAT IS GINGER BEER?   80
FRESH HERBS   87
WHAT IS VERJUICE?   90
TOMATO WATER AND TOMATO JUICE   100

FALL   111

Autumn Apple   115
Hot Buttered Rum   119
PomIranian   123
Bella Ruffina   125
Grapes of Roth   127
Irian Jaya   131
Lemongrass Lemonade   133
Painful Punch   135

DEHYDRATING FRUIT   113
MARASCHINO LIQUEUR AND AMARENA
    CHERRIES   121
EDIBLE FLOWERS   129

Meet the Farmers   136
Meet the Distillers   143
Index   147

ACKNOWLEDGMENTS

My deepest gratitude to:

My family, for always being supportive.

My gurus, Nick Peyton and Douglas Keane, for giving me my dream job and letting me run with it.

Drew Glassel, Rachel Sillcocks, Annie Clemmons, Suzanne Popick, Jeff Talbot, and the cooks at Cyrus, for allowing me into your kitchen, even when you were very busy (when are you not?), and taking time to answer my persistent questions about cooking and exotic ingredients.

Kelly Sullivan, for being my other half at the bar . . . none of this would have been possible without you.

The Cyrus staff working in the main dining room, for taking the time to encourage your guests to try these crazy drinks when we all know it is much easier to sell Champagne.

Sara Remington, Nissa Quanstrom, Peggi Jeung, Julie Bennett, and Toni Tajima for being so patient with this here first-timer.

Brigid Finley and everyone at Wagstaff Worldwide, for helping me get my name out there.

Carole Bidnick, for taking me on, helping me make this book happen, and guiding me through the process.

The writers who were good enough to generate enough press about the bar at Cyrus to warrant interest in a book: Joy Alferness, Michael Bauer, Amanda Berne, Matt Bloom, Anthony Dias Blue, John Bonné, Virginie Boone, Rob Costantino and everyone at *Santé* magazine, Camper English, Marcia Gagliardi, Jenn Garbee, Scott Hocker, Heather John, Michele Anna Jordan,

Jeffery Lindenmuth, Jordan MacKay, Christie Matheson, James Meehan, Linda Murphy, Gary and Mardee Regan, Ruth Reichl, James Rodewald, Josh Sens, Sarah Sung, Patricia Unterman, Molly Watson, Will Welch, and Rob Willey.

The bartenders and chefs who have inspired and influenced me: Tony Abou-Ganim, Eric Adkins, Scott Baird, Joel Baker, Jacques Bezuidenhout, Dale DeGroff, Michael Denton, Marcovaldo Dionysos, Michael Ellis, Michael English, Jeff Hollinger, Eric Johnson, Yanni Kehagiaras, Thomas Keller, Camber Lay, Kevin McCann, Patrick McCluskey, Duggan McDonnell, Paul McManus, Franz Meis, Brian Miller, Dave Nepove, Kurt Niver, Daniel Patterson, Sasha Petraske, Johnny Raglin, Rian Rinn, Audrey Saunders, Rob Schwartz, Todd Smith, Dominic Venegas, Thad Volger, Phil Ward, Alice Waters, Thomas Waugh, Neyah White, and Kevin Young.

Mary Kelly and everyone who sells at the Healdsburg Farmers' Markets.

Michael Pollan, for writing books that have forced me to think about everything I put in my mouth, where it came from, how it was raised, and how it got delivered to my plate or glass.

BOURBON WHISKEY

TO BE CALLED BOURBON IT DOESN'T HAVE TO
ENTUCKY. BOURBON COUNTY WAS THE LA
Y TO OTHER PLACES BACK IN THE EARLY 19
6, 1960). THE LEGAL CRITERIA FOR A S
PRODUCED FOR U.S. BOURBON PRODUCED

INTRODUCTION
Drinks Inspired by the Seasons

LOCATED just off the town square in Healdsburg, California, Cyrus Restaurant sits in the heart of a rich agricultural landscape where organic farmers, small dairies, artisan cheese makers, specialty meat purveyors, and premier vineyards produce some of the finest food and wine in the world. It is easy to be inspired with so many high-quality, local ingredients bursting from the earth.

However, when I first started tending bar in the late 1990s, the definition of an exotic cocktail was artificially flavored liqueur mixed with vodka or rum, and juice. These drinks were generally oversized, full of sugar, high in alcohol content, and far from what I would consider a quality beverage. Since I was new to the business of bartending, I was only concerned about mastering the techniques of preparing the ubiquitous cosmopolitan and a lemon drop with Chambord floating at the bottom. But about two years into my bar career, I ordered a drink from bartender Marco Dionysos at San Francisco's Absinthe Brasserie & Bar that would radically change my perspective.

For the cocktail program at Absinthe, Marco designed many original drinks and resurrected a few dozen recipes from classic cocktail books and magazines; his Ginger Rogers was a perfect blend of gin, mint, lime juice, house-made ginger syrup, and soda. It was unlike anything I'd ever tasted, tart and refreshing, with muddled fresh herbs. Marco had cooked up his own fresh ginger syrup, and I could actually taste the spicy ginger root in the finish. He had been bold enough to make the drink with gin instead of vodka, and this in and of itself was a revelation to me. I knew after those first few sips that I wanted to make drinks that tasted like that Ginger Rogers. The drink reminded me of flavors I had grown up with but had never tasted in a cocktail before.

In Search of Ginger Rogers

I was lucky to have been born and raised in San Francisco, where exotic cuisines are served on just about every street corner. My earliest memories are spiced with the flavors and aromas of traditional Asian, Indian, and Latin American dishes characterized by hearty doses of citrus, spice, and chiles. I've always relished the challenge of trying to identify unfamiliar ingredients in a dish, especially when the flavors are layered and complex. After tasting the Ginger Rogers, I decided to turn that attention to cocktails.

As I began my efforts to create cocktails with more dimension than the ones I had been making in my early bartending career, I realized that my drinks would only be memorable if I obtained specialty produce from international markets and taught myself how to process the ingredients for use in a drink rather than food. I had lots of ideas, but I was still learning about the bar business. I shared my newfound enthusiasm with my managers as well as patrons—and quickly learned that cocktail programs exist to make money for the restaurant, and customers generally want their usual drink. This was going to be harder than I thought, but I was still inspired by the fresh flavors of that Ginger Rogers.

I began to read books about classic cocktails and started hanging out in high-quality cocktail bars around the Bay Area—all in the name of research, of course. I wandered the alleyways of San Francisco's Chinatown buying little packages of spices that I'd never heard of, bottles of liquid without a single word of English on the label, and exotic-looking produce that I'd never seen before. Many of these rare fruits, fresh herbs, and dried spices were expensive and difficult to obtain consistently. None of my bosses was interested in bankrolling my experimental endeavors, and to be honest, the results were hardly notable. Like any beginner, I made mistakes, burned things to a crisp, and wasted a lot of product on combinations that didn't work. But I had an abundance of passion, and even though I poured a lot of my own money down the drain, I learned something valuable from every mistake.

All of this experimentation meant that I often found myself in need of commercial kitchen equipment that I didn't have at home. Bartenders were hardly a welcome sight in the kitchens of the restaurants where I worked, since the cooks were inevitably scrambling to prepare for each evening's food service. After a few stressful confrontations, I reverted to experimenting at home with the equipment I had, all the while waiting for an opportunity to work at a restaurant that would allow me some creative freedom.

The Bar at Cyrus

This opportunity arrived in 2004 when I met legendary maître d' Nick Peyton and then rising star chef Douglas Keane. Nick and Douglas were getting ready to open an upscale destination restaurant in the heart of the Sonoma wine country, and I had moved to Napa Valley a few years before. After tasting some of the drinks I had created with my partners in the bar at St. Helena's Martini House, Nick and Douglas offered me the bar manager position at Cyrus, which was scheduled to open a year later.

Seeing an opportunity to finally take a new approach to cocktails, I shared with Nick and Douglas my vision of a bar stocked with carefully selected spirits and fresh ingredients. To my amazement, they told me I could design the Cyrus bar program however I wanted as long as the costs matched the budget and the response from our guests was positive.

I spent months researching and choosing the finest bottles of liquor for the bar, and I wrote a forty-page spirits menu that described each and every one. I used only fresh-squeezed juices and house-made syrups, and I offered new twists on several classics, including a Manhattan and a Sazerac. The initial response to my drinks was favorable, but once I took a careful look at the incredible food coming out of Douglas's kitchen, I started to feel a little unsettled.

Only a few weeks after opening, Cyrus was being compared to Thomas Keller's French Laundry. The flexible, multicourse, contemporary luxury experience that Nick and Douglas had spent years planning was a huge hit. The elegant ambiance, carefully choreographed service, extensive wine program, and perfect cuisine were dazzling guests, and the reviews reflected this. Even though no one complained about the cocktails, I felt that my contribution to the restaurant was average by comparison.

I started spending a lot of time at Healdsburg's two weekly farmers' markets, getting to know the people who grew the ingredients I was using. I soon learned that Healdsburg had one of California's first farmers' markets, established in the 1970s. Almost every vendor at the market lives and farms within about a fifteen-mile radius of town, and I found myself seeing many of them at the market in the morning, at the coffee shop in the afternoon, and sometimes at one of the local bars after work. Many of the farmers are retired folks supplementing their income or people who have a little piece of land they utilize part time. For others, farming is their livelihood and is intimately intertwined with their philosophy of eating organic, locally produced food.

One day I asked Ron and Bibiana Love of Love Farms if I could visit their farm and discuss what they might start growing for the next season. They agreed, and soon I was stopping by Love Farms, which is located only blocks from Cyrus, every day to gather what I needed for service that night. The more I visited the farms, the more I began to understand about the life cycles of plants and when each one generates the best leaves, buds, and flowers. I started incorporating this new knowledge into my cocktails in different ways. For example, I not only used four kinds of basil in my drinks, but I also used each type's beautiful buds and tiny basil flowers as garnishes.

In addition to dozens of varieties of herbs, I had daily access to an amazing bounty of edible flowers. These fresh herbs and flowers proved to be the missing component in my cocktail program. While I was getting better and better at learning how to process each ingredient for use in drinks (thanks in large part to a very friendly and helpful kitchen staff), the extra little touches like fresh flowers and herbs made the drinks visually stunning. The drinks were getting noticed by our guests. From this point on, I knew that to make the cocktail program truly special, I would have to take some extra time each day to make sure we had these special ingredients at the bar.

As the cocktail program gained recognition, I made more and more friends in town. I made a deal with the owner of the local Chevy dealership to trade his Meyer lemons and satsuma mandarins for restaurant credit. And once word got out that a local bartender was trading restaurant credit for produce, more offers came in the form of peaches, Asian pears, apples, pomegranates, and many varieties of citrus. In addition to securing goods from local farmers, I soon discovered that many ingredients could be foraged from the woods nearby, including blackberries, huckleberries, elderberries, wild fennel, and miner's lettuce. To complement the local ingredients, I started using spirits born in the San Francisco Bay Area, too. Domaine Charbay, St. George Spirits (Hangar One), Germain Robin, Anchor Distillery, and others produce some of the finest spirits on the planet. Taking full advantage of this bounty has become a year-round undertaking and my greatest passion.

Artisanal Cocktails

My hope with these recipes is to inspire. I've spent my life immersed in the culinary traditions of Northern California, and these cocktails have sprung from my exposure to the exciting flavors and aromas I've experienced in this area's restaurants. I've organized this book by season because that's how we run the bar program at Cyrus: cocktails appear on the menu when their ingredients are in season, then drop off the menu when the ingredients disappear.

For me, the challenge has been translating flavor combinations that work well in food into successful drinks. To save you the trouble of experimenting like I did, I've included lots of culinary tips and techniques that can be applied to cocktails in countless ways.

Cocktails that are strained into martini glasses are classically garnished with a maraschino cherry or with a fruit wedge stuck on the rim. In attempting to add more drama to my cocktails, I've added foams, dehydrated fruit, and pickled and candied treats, along with fresh herbs and edible flowers. And instead of muddling whole fresh herbs in the bottom of the mixing glass, I sometimes chop them into a chiffonade, which releases their flavor as well as muddling does but also creates beautiful thin strips of herb that wrap attractively around pieces of ice. For each season of drinks, there are particularly relevant techniques, such as how to properly juice, strain, and store citrus in the winter or how to make the world's best pickling liquid for wonderful onions in the spring. Once you learn these techniques, you can use them as a base from which to do your own experimenting.

A WORD ABOUT ICE

Although it might not seem like a big deal, using the correct ice for cocktails is critical. For instance, the Mint Julep (page 85) tastes best served over crushed ice, and the Frankfort Manhattan (page 65) should be stirred with large cubes (see "Perfect Ice Cubes" on page 58). Most of the cocktails in this book, however, are either shaken and strained into a V-shaped glass or served tall with lots of edible ingredients clinging dramatically to the ice. In both of these cases, small cubed ice is highly recommended to achieve the best results.

I don't recommend using ice made in a refrigerator ice machine or in ice cube trays. These cubes are generally too large and they tend to pick up the flavors of food, especially meat, stored in your freezer. You certainly don't want the flavor of frozen chicken in your margarita—and believe me when I tell you that the meat flavor only gets more intense as the ice melts. So, if you don't happen to work in a restaurant, where do you get the right kind of ice for these drinks? You could either make a deal with your neighborhood bar or restaurant to buy ice from their professional ice machine, or in a pinch you could buy bagged ice from the store and break it into small cubes using the stainless steel part of a Boston Shaker.

While certain drinks will require an old-fashioned glass or champagne flute, most of my cocktails are served in either a 12-ounce tall collins glass or a 7-ounce V-shaped (martini) glass. For mixing drinks, I have always preferred the Boston Shaker, which is basically a pint-sized beer glass with a slightly larger stainless steel cup that fits snugly on top when given a firm tap. I place all of the ingredients in this 16-ounce mixing glass and stir them well, without ice, before shaking or serving. Each cocktail contains 3 to 3 1/2 ounces of liquor and juice before the rest of the ingredients and ice are added. Once I add the rest of the ingredients and the ice, I shake the drink and either strain or pour it into the glass.

Cocktails served in a tall collins glass must have a full measure of ice (enough to fill the glass) added after the drink has been stirred. This is so the pieces of fresh herbs, fruit, and flowers will cling to the ice, be evenly dispersed, and look fantastic when dumped into the glass. By adding this amount of ice to the glass, the cocktail stays colder longer and dilutes less. The measures should be exact as we're playing a game of displacement with the 3 to 3 1/2 ounces of liquid, the 16-ounce mixing glass, and the ice. After you shake the drink a few times and pour everything into a 12-ounce collins glass, the drink should fit almost exactly. Just make sure you don't shake these drinks too hard, or you'll bruise or break the edible parts in the mixing glass.

Cocktails presented in a V-shaped glass also get a full measure of ice added to the mixing glass after the ingredients have been stirred well. The purpose of shaking these drinks is to chill and slightly dilute the cocktail, not to mix it, as it has already been stirred. I shake the drink hard for about seven seconds, then strain it into the glass. With many of my cocktails, I like to add a layer of foam to the top after straining, as well as pieces of dehydrated fruit or edible flowers for garnish. These finishing touches are optional, of course, but they make the cocktail look extraordinary. And if the cocktail looks beautiful, your mind believes it will taste good even before you take your first sip. If you can actually make it taste great, you've got a winner.

The recipes in this book generally yield one drink because, for the most part, these drinks have to be created one at a time. You can prepare certain ingredients ahead of time, which makes it easy to mix up a drink or two or a whole party's worth of cocktails, depending on the occasion. If you've had the good fortune of dining at Cyrus, you may recognize many of these drinks from the bar there, and you'll notice some new concoctions as well. I'm constantly experimenting with new ingredients, and I encourage you to do the same. The cocktails in this book embrace my philosophy of using peak-of-season, locally produced ingredients. When you are making drinks, I encourage you to do the same, whether by enjoying the bounty of your own garden, becoming friends with a farmer, or buying ingredients at organic or farmers' markets. These drinks take time to prepare, but I've found that the process can be as enjoyable as that first sip. Cheers!

CHAPTER 1

WINTER

W H E N the weather turns gray and rainy and the farmers' markets close, you might think a seasonally minded bartender like myself would face a dearth of ingredients to get through the winter. But the opposite is actually the case: in addition to being world-class wine regions, Northern California's Napa and Sonoma counties happen to have perfect citrus-growing weather. It's hot during summer and fall, generally with few periods of below-freezing temperatures in winter and spring. This makes winter an exciting time of year for cocktails.

Fresh-squeezed citrus juices make deliciously tart and refreshing cocktails, not unlike the Ginger Rogers that originally inspired me. After moving to Healdsburg, I noticed an abundance of citrus trees growing in people's front yards and decided to knock on a few doors to see if anyone was up for a trade. They were, and today almost all of the citrus that we use at Cyrus from late fall to late winter is bartered to us from friends who live in Healdsburg and the neighboring Dry Creek Valley.

Ruby Red grapefruits; Meyer and Eureka lemons; Rangpur and Key limes; bergamot, Valencia, and blood oranges; and satsuma mandarins are dropped off by our neighbors or picked by us almost daily. The preparation of these fruits, the foundation of our winter cocktails, is described in the coming pages. Foams, salted and sugared rims, and spiced sugar syrups are complementary to high-acid drinks and thus are also described in this chapter.

Even when the weather is cold and gloomy, the refreshing bite of a midwinter citrus cocktail will remind you that warm and sunny days are right around the corner.

THE IMPORTANCE OF PROPER JUICING

Yes, it's possible to buy "freshly squeezed" citrus juice in your local grocery store, but bottled juice doesn't come close to matching the quality and flavor of juice squeezed straight out of the fruit into your glass. Although flash-pasteurization might make fruit juice safer to drink if it has to sit on a truck while being shipped around the country to further sit on grocery store shelves, many of the subtle nuances of the juice will be gone by the time you open the container. And like a bottle of recently opened wine, fruit juice begins to lose its flavor as soon as it's squeezed. That's why the best cocktails are made from fruit that you juice and use right away. When citrus fruit is freshly squeezed, the brightly acidic and sweet juice and richly flavored essential oils combine to produce an ideal ingredient for great cocktails. The taste of juice from peak-of-season, fresh-picked fruit is unmistakable.

Available seasonally, unwaxed citrus is ideal for juicing. When you buy citrus fruit from a conventional grocery store, it has a thin layer of wax sprayed onto it to preserve it and make it shiny. While this wax isn't going to hurt you or taste bad, unwaxed citrus purchased from a local farmer in season is always going to taste better. If you do buy your produce from a conventional grocery store, give your citrus a light scrub with a plastic brush and always rinse it well before juicing. Since more juice can be extracted from room-temperature citrus than from citrus fresh from the refrigerator, let the fruit sit on your counter for a few hours before juicing.

If you're using a hand squeezer, press and roll the fruit on a hard surface with the palm of your hand a few times before squeezing. This softens the fruit and makes hand squeezing more effective. If you are fortunate enough to have a pull-down or electric juicer, you can eliminate this step; these devices are highly effective at extracting all of the juice.

Strain the juice through a fine-mesh strainer or chinois to remove any pulp or seeds. Be sure to store the juice in an airtight container in the refrigerator and discard it after forty-eight hours. You can certainly use refrigerated juices more than two days old either straight or in a lemonade or limeade, but only use the freshest juice for cocktails.

I applaud bartenders who squeeze fresh citrus to order, but in practice the cocktails can be inconsistent due to the variance of juice from each piece of fruit. When mixing cocktails, it's paramount to measure the amount of juice (and other liquid ingredients) accurately. I use a jigger to measure out the juice. After straining the pulp and seeds from the juice, I pour it into a squeeze bottle because it makes assembling cocktails easier. I cut off half of the bottle's plastic tip to allow a bigger flow of juice with each squeeze. (I also use squeeze bottles to dispense simple syrups; see page 20.)

HELLO CELLO

MAKES 2 (750 ML) BOTTLES

A traditional drink in certain parts of Italy, most famously the Amalfi coast, limoncello is typically made from winter citrus but enjoyed all year long. There are many ways to make a cello. My preferred method is to combine 100-proof vodka infused with citrus peel and simple syrup at a two-to-one ratio. I juice a lot of citrus at the bar but don't like to throw away the beautiful skins. This basic cello recipe gives me an excuse to use the whole fruit. Feel free to use limes, oranges, or grapefruits, or a combination of two or more. If you can't get local, unwaxed citrus, give it a good scrubbing before zesting. Cellos make fabulous presents for the holidays and are relatively inexpensive to make, especially if you have a citrus tree in your yard. Don't waste your money on expensive brands of vodka for this recipe; I usually use 100-proof Smirnoff. Store cello in the freezer and serve it in a frozen glass.

8 lemons, 10 limes, 4 grapefruits, 6 oranges, or a combination
1 quart 100-proof vodka
2 cups simple syrup (see page 20)

USING a potato peeler or a sharp paring knife, zest the citrus fruit over and into a large airtight container until you have approximately $1\frac{1}{3}$ cups of zest. Try to avoid zesting the white pith, which is bitter. Pour the vodka into the container. Cover and let the vodka and zest mixture rest for at least 1 week in a cool, dark place. Once infused, strain out the zest and add the simple syrup to the vodka. Seal the container and let the cello rest for 1 more week, refrigerated. Strain the cello into glass bottles and store them in the freezer.

Variation: I like to enhance my simple syrups with essential oils (see page 21) before mixing them into the infused vodka. One or two drops per pint of simple syrup will do the trick. Some of my favorite combinations are star anise syrup with grapefruit cello, bergamot syrup with orange cello, and ginger syrup with lime cello. Feel free to experiment.

MEYER BEAUTIFUL (MY, YOU'RE BEAUTIFUL)

MAKES 1 COCKTAIL (see photo on page 14)

This is a tart cocktail that explores the complex flavors of Meyer lemons and elderflowers. Elderflowers have a lovely lychee aroma and flavor that marries well with the citrus-floral tones of Meyer lemons. Before you taste your first sip, the sugar, black salt, and lemon zest rim wake up your mouth. Late season Meyers can be rather sweet, so when they lack acid I substitute juice from regular Eureka lemons for half of the lemon juice.

Dried zest of 1 large or 2 small Meyer lemons, for rim

5 tablespoons sugar, for rim

1 tablespoon black sea salt, for rim (optional)

1/2 Meyer lemon, for rim

1 egg white

1 ounce Charbay Meyer lemon vodka

1 ounce vodka

3/4 ounce freshly squeezed Meyer lemon juice

1/2 ounce D'arbo elderflower syrup

Baked Candied Meyer Lemon Peels, for garnish

Edible flowers, for garnish (optional)

PLACE a V-shaped glass in the freezer to chill. Preheat the oven to 375°F. Follow the recipe on page 19 to make Candied Meyer Lemon Peels. Shake off any excess syrup and slice the peels into thin strips. Line a baking sheet with a silicone mat and arrange the strips so they don't touch. Bake for 5 minutes, remove from the oven, and let cool to room temperature. If they aren't hard and devoid of moisture when cool, bake for 2 minutes more.

Combine the zest, sugar, and salt on a small plate. Rub the Meyer lemon half around the rim of the chilled glass and shake off any excess juice. Dip the glass into the sugar-zest mixture to coat the rim (see page 38).

Place the egg white in a mixing glass (see page 30), seal it up tight with a firm tap, and shake vigorously for 10 seconds, until white and frothy. Add the vodkas, juice, syrup, and enough ice to fill the glass. Cover and shake vigorously for another 10 seconds. Strain into the sugar-rimmed glass. After about 20 seconds, a nice head will form on top of the drink. Garnish with the candied zest, edible flowers, or both to serve.

Clockwise from top: Bleeding Orange (page 26),
Pelo Del Perro, and Meyer Beautiful (page 13).

PELO DEL PERRO (HAIR OF THE DOG)

MAKES 1 COCKTAIL

I originally designed this drink as a hangover remedy. The juices provide lots of vitamin C, the agave nectar adds natural fructose, and 500 micrograms of vitamin B_{12} will wake up the weary. The powdered form of vitamin B_{12} is easiest to use, but if you can only find pills, just muddle the pill into a powder before adding the other ingredients. Despite being an effective morning-after cocktail, the Pelo del Perro is also a beautiful pink and red drink with sweet, salty, and tangy flavors woven through a silky grapefruit foam.

Grapefruit foam, for garnish (see page 28)

$1/2$ grapefruit or blood orange, for rim

1 tablespoon pink sea salt, for rim

5 tablespoons sugar, for rim

500 micrograms B_{12} powder

$1/2$ ounce Charbay Ruby Red grapefruit vodka

$1/2$ ounce vodka

$1/2$ ounce 100 percent agave silver (plata) tequila

$1/2$ ounce freshly squeezed grapefruit juice

$1/2$ ounce freshly squeezed lime juice

$1/4$ ounce agave nectar

Dianthus or other edible flower petals, for garnish

PLACE a V-shaped glass in the freezer to chill. Follow the instructions on page 29 to prepare and chill the grapefruit foam using grapefruit juice as the base.

Rub the grapefruit half around the rim of the frozen glass and shake off any excess juice. Dip the glass into the sea salt and sugar to coat the rim (see page 38). Toss the B_{12} powder in a measuring glass and add the liquors, juices, and agave nectar. Stir well and add enough ice to fill the glass. Shake hard for 7 seconds and strain into the salt-rimmed glass. Add a thin layer of grapefruit foam on top. Garnish with a few dianthus or other edible flower petals to serve.

Variation: Mix dried grapefruit zest with red sea salt and sugar before you rim the glass.

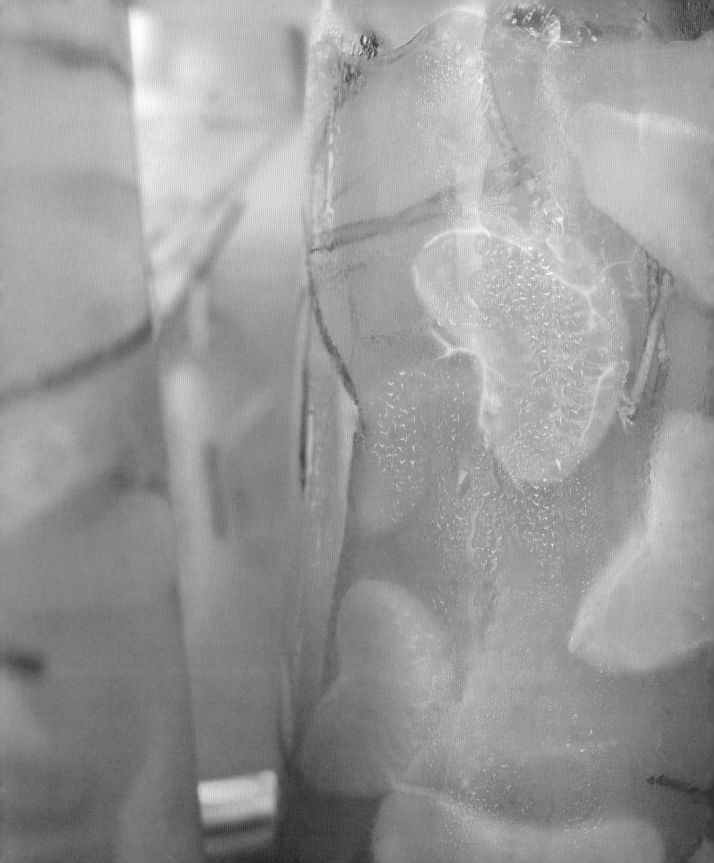

WAVERLY PLACE ECHO

MAKES 1 COCKTAIL

Waverly Place is my favorite alleyway in San Francisco's Chinatown, where late at night you can hear the loud smacking of mah-jongg tiles echoing off the walls above the deserted street. The flavors in this drink are Chinese inspired, featuring hints of mandarin orange, star anise, and Szechuan peppercorns. These special peppercorns—available at Asian markets—are actually not peppercorns at all. They come from the flowering *sancho* plant, and when dried and toasted are flavorful and aromatic with hints of citrus zest and spice. The mandarin orange segments marinated in five-spice simple syrup are an extra treat to be snacked on while enjoying this refreshing cocktail. My good friend Bruce McConnell and his family grow Meyer lemons and satsuma mandarins for Cyrus throughout the winter (for which we trade restaurant credit). Bartering never tasted so good.

3/4 ounce Hangar One mandarin orange blossom vodka

3/4 ounce vodka

6 Five-Spice Marinated Mandarin Orange Segments (see recipe)

1 ounce freshly squeezed Meyer lemon juice

5 to 6 Candied Meyer Lemon Peels (see recipe)

1/2 ounce Chinese Five-Spice Syrup (see recipe)

3 Kaffir lime leaves, cut into long chiffonade

3/4 ounce seltzer

IN a mixing glass, combine the vodkas, mandarin segments, lemon juice, candied peels, syrup, lime leaves, and seltzer. Stir everything around a bit, add a full measure of ice, and shake a few times. Pour the contents into a tall collins glass to serve.

continued

Chinese Five-Spice Syrup

MAKES 2²/₃ CUPS (ENOUGH FOR ABOUT 25 COCKTAILS AND 30 MARINATED MANDARIN ORANGE SEGMENTS

5 whole star anise pods

1 tablespoon fennel seeds

1 (3-inch) cinnamon stick, broken into
   pieces

1 teaspoon whole cloves

1 tablespoon Szechuan peppercorns

2²/₃ cups simple syrup (see page 20)

2 teaspoons honey

To make the syrup, process the spices to a coarse powder in a spice or coffee grinder. Heat a stainless steel pot over medium heat, add the spices, and follow the instructions on page 20 to toast the spices. Once fragrant, add the simple syrup to the pan and bring to a boil. Reduce the heat to low and add the honey. Simmer for 5 minutes to infuse the syrup mixture with the flavor of the spices, then remove from the heat. Let the mixture cool to at least room temperature, then strain it through a fine-mesh strainer or chinois to remove any solids. The syrup will keep for up to 1 month if refrigerated in an airtight container.

Five-Spice Marinated Mandarin Orange Segments

MAKES 30 SEGMENTS (ENOUGH FOR 5 COCKTAILS)

> 5 satsuma mandarins
>
> 1 cup Chinese Five-Spice Syrup (see recipe), at room temperature

Remove the outer peel of the mandarin and any white stringy matter clinging to the fruit. Separate the segments and place them in a bowl with the syrup. Let them marinate for at least 15 minutes before using. The segments will last for about 1 week if kept refrigerated in an airtight container.

Candied Meyer Lemon Peels

MAKES ABOUT 5 PEELS (ENOUGH FOR 1 COCKTAIL)

> 1 large Meyer lemon
>
> 1/2 cup simple syrup

Using a potato peeler or a sharp paring knife, remove the zest from the lemon in long, wide pieces from the top of the lemon to the bottom; I usually get about five pieces of peel per lemon, but be aware that Meyer lemons can vary quite a bit in size. Avoid the white bitter pith as much as possible. Use the lemon for the freshly squeezed juice called for above. Heat the simple syrup in a stainless steel pan over high heat until it boils. Add the peels, bring the syrup back up to a boil, then reduce the heat to low and simmer for 5 minutes. Let the syrup and peels cool to at least room temperature before using. The peels will last for up to 1 week stored in the syrup in an airtight container and refrigerated.

SPICED SIMPLE SYRUPS

Infusing a drink with the flavor of your favorite spice is remarkably easy. There are two ways to go about this. The first is to heat ground spices in a pan until aromatic, add a syrup or juice to the pan, and simmer until the spice infuses the liquid. The second is to add a few drops of essential oil to a liquid. They both work equally well, but essential oils tend to be quicker and easier to work with, and also less expensive because a little goes a long way. If you are going to be making more than just a few cocktails at a time, dispensing the simple syrup from a squeeze bottle is the easiest, cleanest, and most efficient way to go (see page 11).

To make simple syrup:

1. Combine equal parts of boiling water and superfine granulated sugar. The final yield of simple syrup is the same as the starting measurement of the water.
2. Stir well until the sugar is completely dissolved.
3. Store in an airtight container in the refrigerator for up to 1 month.

To toast whole spices:

1. To infuse 1 cup of simple syrup or other liquid, use a spice or coffee grinder to grind enough whole, dry spice (or a combination of spices) to give you 4 teaspoons of coarse powder. (To infuse different amounts of liquid, use this same ratio of 4 teaspoons per cup of liquid, or $^{1}/_{3}$ cup spice per quart of liquid.)
2. Heat a sufficiently large stainless steel pan over medium heat and toss in the ground spices.
3. Shake the pan to distribute the spices in an even layer and cook until little wisps of smoke rise up. This usually takes only a few seconds. Remove the pan from the heat, shaking and tossing the spices repeatedly. They should be aromatic, but be careful not to burn them.
4. Return the pan to the heat, cook until little wisps of smoke rise up again, then remove from

the heat, and shake and toss the spices. Repeat this step three more times, or until the spices are very aromatic.

To infuse simple syrup with toasted spices:

1. Return the pan of toasted spices to the heat and add 1 cup of simple syrup. Increase the heat to high and bring the mixture to a boil, then reduce the heat to low and simmer for 5 minutes. Remove the pan from the heat.
2. Let the spice mixture rest in the pan for 1 hour, then strain it through a fine-mesh strainer or chinois and allow it to cool to a least room temperature before use.

These syrups will keep for weeks if refrigerated in an airtight container.

Essential oils are 100 percent natural, organic materials that have been steam distilled. It generally takes only a few drops to enhance a quart of simple syrup, puree, or juice, which makes essential oils cheaper to use than whole ground spices. However, each essential oil is different, which means sometimes you'll only need 1 drop per quart of liquid and other times you'll need 30 drops per quart. They will not disperse in water, which is why you should always infuse a syrup, puree, or juice. You should never use even one drop of essential oil directly in a drink or in the mouth, as it will overwhelm your palate and taste horrible. Pregnant women shouldn't consume drinks with certain essential oils in them, and although essential oils are natural and organic, they are concentrated and shouldn't be put directly on the skin or in the eyes. I buy mine online at www.libertynatural.com.

To infuse a syrup with essential oil:

1. Combine 3 cups of chilled simple syrup with 1 to 2 drops of essential oil in an airtight container.
2. Cover and shake well.
3. If the flavor seems weak, add 1 to 2 drops more, cover, and shake again.

The syrup will keep for 3 to 4 weeks refrigerated in the airtight container.

LOTUS POTION

MAKES 1 COCKTAIL

Dan and Laura Sooy, who live down the street from me in Healdsburg, have two huge orange trees, as well as a rare decades-old Rangpur lime tree that we utilize for the Hot Indian Date (page 35). One of the orange trees produces small, tart oranges perfect for high-acid cocktails, and the other yields large, sweet fruits better for drinking with eggs and ham. The Lotus Potion has many of the flavors found in the Waverly Place Echo (page 17), but here they have been translated into a very different drink served in a V-shaped glass. A crisp, pink lotus chip and late-winter purple rosemary blossoms make beautiful garnishes atop orange foam. Note that it takes a couple of days to stain and dehydrate the lotus chips, so plan ahead when making this cocktail.

Orange foam, for garnish (see page 28)

3/4 ounce Hangar One mandarin orange blossom vodka

3/4 ounce vodka

1/2 ounce freshly squeezed orange juice

3/4 ounce freshly squeezed Meyer lemon juice

1/4 ounce Chinese Five-Spice Syrup (page 18)

2 dashes orange bitters

1 Crispy Lotus Root Chip, for garnish (see recipe)

Rosemary blossoms or other edible purple flowers, for garnish

PLACE a V-shaped glass in the freezer to chill. Follow the instructions on page 29 to prepare and chill the orange foam using orange juice as the base.

In a mixing glass, combine the vodkas, juices, syrup, and bitters. Give it all a stir and add enough ice to fill the glass. Cover and shake hard for 7 seconds. Strain into the chilled glass and apply a thin layer of orange foam on top. Set the lotus chip in the center of the foam and surround it with the rosemary blossoms.

continued

Crispy Lotus Root Chips

....

MAKES ABOUT 15 CHIPS (ENOUGH FOR 15 DRINKS)

1 vanilla bean

1/2 cup sugar

1 (5-inch) lotus root

1 cup simple syrup (see page 20)

1 small red beet, cooked and peeled

Using a sharp knife, split the vanilla bean open along the long edge. Place the bean in the sugar and let it sit for 24 hours. Remove the bean and stir the sugar.

Peel the lotus root with a potato peeler. Using a mandoline or very sharp knife, slice the root paper-thin or as thin as you can. Set a saucepan with 1 quart of water over high heat until it boils. Remove the pan from the heat and place the lotus chips in the water for 15 seconds to blanch. Strain the lotus chips out of the water and set aside.

In a saucepan, bring the simple syrup to a boil over high heat. Cut the beet into about 5 slices and add it to the syrup. Remove the pan from the heat, pour the contents into an airtight container, and carefully add the lotus pieces to the syrup. Allow the syrup to cool, then cover it and place it in the refrigerator for 24 hours, stirring the mixture gently a few times to distribute the color evenly. Depending on how red the beet is, the lotus pieces will become pink to red. If you want a redder color, leave them in longer.

I use a food dehydrator to make the chips crispy; you could also bake them at a very low temperature in the oven. If using a food dehydrator, spray the trays with vegetable oil or lightly oil them with a paper towel. Lay the lotus root slices on the trays. Sprinkle each slice with a little bit of the vanilla sugar. Dehydrating will take 24 to 36 hours, depending on the thickness of the slice (see page 113); let the slices dehydrate until very dry and crispy.

If using the oven, preheat it to 150°F (if you use a higher temperature the chips will turn brown). Lay the lotus root slices on a silicone mat and sprinkle each with a little bit of the vanilla sugar. Place the silicone mat on the center rack in the oven and bake for 5 hours, until almost all of the moisture is gone. Set the chips on a wire rack to cool. They will be warm, soft, and limp for a few minutes and will harden as they cool, just like cookies fresh from the oven. If they're still moist after cooling, bake them for 30 minutes more. Stored in an airtight container, the chips will keep for 2 to 3 days.

BLEEDING ORANGE

MAKES 1 COCKTAIL (see photo on page 14)

This cocktail combines the flavors, colors, and aromas I associate with winter: Meyer lemons, blood oranges, cinnamon, nutmeg, and allspice. The cocktail is a vibrant red, provided you have access to the dark red blood oranges that sometimes appear only later in the season. The rim is flecked with spices as well as sugar and orange zest. Tart, spicy, sweet, and made from fruit-enhanced vodkas and fresh fruit juice—this drink must be good for you.

$^1/_2$ blood orange, for rim

Winter Spice-Orange Sugar, for rim (see recipe)

$^1/_2$ ounce Charbay blood orange vodka

$^1/_2$ ounce Charbay Meyer lemon vodka

$^1/_2$ ounce vodka

$^1/_2$ ounce freshly squeezed Meyer lemon juice

$^1/_2$ ounce freshly squeezed blood orange juice

2 dashes Fee Brothers peach bitters

$^1/_2$ ounce Winter Spice Syrup (see recipe)

Blanketflower petals or other edible flowers, for garnish

PLACE a V-shaped glass in the freezer to chill.

Rub the blood orange half around the rim of the chilled glass and shake off any excess juice. Dip the glass into the spice-sugar mixture to coat the rim (see page 38).

In a mixing glass, combine the vodkas, juices, bitters, and syrup and give it a stir. Add enough ice to fill the glass, shake hard for 7 seconds, and strain into the sugar-rimmed glass to serve.

Winter Spice-Orange Sugar

RIMS ABOUT 30 GLASSES

1 tablespoon ground spice mixture (see Winter Spice Syrup recipe)

5 tablespoons sugar

1 tablespoon blood orange zest, dried (see page 39)

Place the spices, sugar, and zest in a small bowl and stir to combine.

Winter Spice Syrup

....

MAKES ²/₃ CUP (ENOUGH FOR ABOUT 10 COCKTAILS)

> 1 nutmeg pod
>
> 1 (3-inch) cinnamon stick, broken into small pieces
>
> 2 teaspoons whole allspice
>
> ²/₃ cup simple syrup (see page 20)

Place the nutmeg pod in a towel and break it into pieces with a hammer or other blunt object. Place the nutmeg pieces, cinnamon pieces, and allspice in a spice or coffee grinder and process to a coarse powder. Reserve 1 tablespoon of the ground spice mixture for the Winter Spice–Orange Sugar.

Heat a stainless steel pan over medium heat and follow the instructions on page 20 to toast the spices. Add the simple syrup and bring the mixture to a boil over high heat. Reduce the heat to low and simmer for 5 minutes. Remove the spiced syrup from the heat and allow it to cool to room temperature. Pour the syrup through a fine-mesh strainer or chinois to remove any solid pieces. The syrup will keep for 1 month refrigerated in an airtight container.

FOAMS

Foams have been all the rage in fine restaurants for many years, but they have only recently found their way into drink programs. Foams can be savory and rich or fruity and spicy, and may use ingredients from bacon and foie gras to lime and ginger. Basically a liquefied protein-fat combination charged with air bubbles, the silky froth of foams has a wonderful mouthfeel. Most of the foams I use in cocktails have a juice and simple syrup base with a protein-fat combination incorporated into the liquid in stages. A thin layer of foam dispensed on top of a cocktail serves different purposes. If the cocktail is tart, a rich foam adds a nice contrast. It also creates a platform of sorts on top of the drink to support edible flowers, dehydrated fruit slices, a sprinkle of spiced sugar, and other garnishes.

Foams are incredibly fickle, but once you understand the basic concept, there's room for experimentation. The foams in this book begin with 12 ounces of a base with a 3-to-1 ratio of juice to simple syrup. This is heated to a boil but not reduced. If you use gelatin leaves (sheets), you need to soak them in cold water (to "bloom" the leaves) for 10 minutes to bloom the gelatin before adding them to the hot liquid. If you use powdered gelatin, you need to soak it in 3 ounces of the juice or simple syrup (chilled) for 10 minutes to bloom the gelatin before adding it to the hot liquid. Either way, once the gelatin is combined with the base, the mixture needs to cool to at least 45°F before the cold Thai coconut milk is beaten in. Please don't use low-fat coconut milk; you need the fat to produce the proper foam.

The easiest way to charge the foam with air is to use a whipped cream dispenser equipped with nitrous oxide canisters (available at kitchen and restaurant supply stores and from online merchants). The canister should be shaken well before each use and kept in the refrigerator when not dispensing the foam. Foams will stabilize better after they've been charged for 24 hours and left in the refrigerator. Foams always have to be refrigerated and shaken well before each use. If the foam is too thick, try using less gelatin next time. If it is too thin and runny, use more gelatin.

There are many ways to make foams but the following method has never let me down.

Juice-Based Foams

MAKES 2 CUPS (ENOUGH FOR ABOUT 20 COCKTAILS)

1¼ leaves gelatin

4 cups cold water

9 ounces strained fruit juice

3 ounces simple syrup (see page 20)

⅓ cup Thai coconut milk

1. In a metal bowl, bloom the gelatin leaves in the water for 10 minutes.
2. Meanwhile, combine the fruit juice and simple syrup in a small saucepan and heat over medium-high heat just until it boils. Remove the saucepan from the heat.
3. Remove the gelatin from the water and squeeze out most of the excess water. Discard the water and toss the gelatin back into the empty bowl.
4. Fill a large bowl with ice and set the bowl with the gelatin on top of the ice. Pour the hot juice mixture over the gelatin slowly. With a whisk, beat the gelatin until frothy, about 30 seconds.
5. Allow the gelatin mixture to cool to at least 45°F, then whisk in the coconut milk.
6. Pour the mixture into a whipped cream canister and seal it tight. Invert the canister and charge it with a cartridge.
7. Shake the canister vigorously for 15 seconds, then place it in the refrigerator to cool. The foam can be used after about 10 minutes, but it will be more stable after 24 hours. Shake the canister vigorously before each use. Cover the tip of the canister with a small towel so any foam left on the tip from the last use doesn't splatter when you shake it again. Always dispense the foam with the canister completely inverted over the cocktail. If the foam comes out thick, let it settle on top of the drink for 15 to 20 seconds before garnishing. Keep the canister refrigerated when not dispensing the foam.

VARIATION: To use powdered gelatin, combine 1¼ teaspoons of powdered gelatin with 3 ounces of the strained juice or simple syrup, which should be chilled, and allow the gelatin to bloom for 10 minutes. Follow the instructions above to heat the remaining juice and simple syrup mixture. Remove from the heat, add the bloomed gelatin and its soaking liquid, and beat until frothy. Follow the instructions above to cool the mixture, add the coconut milk, and charge the canister.

FOAMS, continued

Egg Whites

Another way to create a very thin layer of foam is to agitate an egg white in a shaker by vigorously shaking it for 10 seconds. Make sure you give the shaker a firm tap to seal it tightly before shaking. After shaking, pour the frothy egg white into the glass portion of the shaker, build your drink on top of it, add ice, seal it, and shake well for another 10 seconds. This method works well for strained drinks served in a V-shaped glass as well as drinks dumped into rocks or tall collins glasses.

Egg whites don't impart much flavor to drinks, but they do bond to citrus juices and sugar to create more texture. Contrary to popular belief, it's safe to consume raw eggs as long as the eggs have been properly sanitized before you use them. (The bacteria that could make you sick are on the outside of the egg and would only come into contact with the egg white when you crack it open.) I rinse my eggs in a solution made from 3 tablespoons of bleach and 9 quarts of cold water. After stirring the mixture well, I carefully lower each egg into the water with tongs or a little wire basket. Then I remove the eggs from the solution, dry each one thoroughly, and store them in the refrigerator until I'm ready to use them.

THAI MONKEY

MAKES 1 COCKTAIL

When the herbs that we use to make the Thai Boxer (page 81) are no longer available from local farms, we take the cocktail off the menu, much to the disappointment of die-hard fans. In an effort to appease these enthusiastic regulars, I created this drink. It is admittedly a very different drink, but it has a similarly complex and refreshing quality. Ginger beer adds some Southeast Asian flavor and a little fizz. Why is it called a Thai Monkey? Well, it contains *Thai* coconut milk, Green Chartreuse (made by *monks*), and a *Key* lime (which are yellow when ripe). And since Thailand has a lot of monkeys, it just seemed to fit.

1 Key lime, cut into 8 pieces

3/4 ounce Hangar One Buddha's hand vodka

3/4 ounce vodka

1/4 ounce Green Chartreuse

1/4 ounce simple syrup (see page 20)

1/2 ounce freshly squeezed Meyer lemon juice

1/2 ounce Thai coconut milk

3/4 ounce Bundaberg or Cock'n Bull ginger beer

3 to 4 thin kiwi slices, for garnish

TOSS the Key lime pieces into a mixing glass and muddle them down well. Add the liquors, lemon juice, coconut milk, and ginger beer, and give it a stir. Add enough ice to fill the mixing glass, cover, and shake a few times. Pour it into two short glasses or a tall collins glass. Top with the kiwi slices to serve.

HOT INDIAN DATE

MAKES 1 COCKTAIL

I love this drink because it is rather sour but has a lingering finish of spice, pickle, and raisin. This might not sound so tasty, but anyone who likes a caipirinha and can handle a little chile will probably enjoy the Hot Indian Date. Rangpur limes (actually a hybrid of mandarin orange and lemon) are difficult to get but well worth tracking down. When the fruit is muddled, its complex bitter oils are released, creating a lingering finish that lasts for minutes. These oils, combined with the tart lime juice, sweet and sour tamarind, chile, and pot-distilled Charbay rum make for a memorable cocktail. You can use many types of hot chiles for the Hot Tamarind Syrup; just add a couple (seeds included) and continue to taste as you add more. There should be a nice burn in the aftertaste.

Canned hearts of palm are available at Asian markets, but I much prefer to use fresh. The thin segments yield beautiful quarter-moon shapes, and the thick parts look like full moons about the size of a silver dollar. You can use either one for this drink, but the quarter-moon pieces look best. The hearts of palm provide a wonderful counterpoint that tempers the spice and sourness of the Hot Indian Date.

1 Rangpur lime, cut into 8 pieces

1 1/2 ounces Charbay or 10 Cane cane rum

1/4 ounce freshly squeezed lime juice

3/4 ounce seltzer

3/4 ounce Hot Tamarind Syrup (see recipe)

5 to 10 pieces Pickled Hearts of Palm (see recipe)

1 small Fresno chile, cut into rings

TOSS the Rangpur lime pieces into a mixing glass and muddle them down well. Add the rum, juice, seltzer, and syrup, and give it a stir. Add enough ice to fill the mixing glass, cover, and shake a few times. Pour it into a tall collins glass and top with the hearts of palm and chile rings (seeds and all). Use a straw or a knife to push the hearts of palm and chile down into the drink so they're evenly dispersed.

continued

Hot Tamarind Syrup

MAKES 2 CUPS (ENOUGH FOR ABOUT 20 COCKTAILS)

1 quart simple syrup (see page 20)

$1/2$ pound tamarind pulp, chopped into small pieces

1 large or 2 small Fresno chiles, cut into rings

1 drop essential oil of cardamom

In a large stainless steel pan over high heat, bring the simple syrup to a boil. Add the tamarind (seeds and all) and bring the mixture back to a boil. Reduce the heat to low and simmer for 20 minutes, or until the tamarind pulp is melted. Add the chiles (seeds and all) and stir. Taste the syrup; if it doesn't have a pleasant burn, stir in some more chile rings. Let the syrup sit for 5 minutes and taste it again, adding more chile if necessary. Strain the mixture through a fine-mesh strainer or chinois into an airtight container. This will involve a bit of elbow grease, as much of the syrup will have to be firmly pressed through the strainer. When there is very little liquid left to be extracted, stop. Scrape off any syrup sticking to the strainer and stir. Let the syrup cool to room temperature, add the essential oil, and stir well. The syrup will keep for about 2 weeks refrigerated in the airtight container.

Pickled Hearts of Palm

MAKES ABOUT 60 PIECES (ENOUGH FOR 6 TO 12 COCKTAILS)

1 pound fresh hearts of palm

3 cups Ultimate Pickling Liquid (page 52)

Set a saucepan with 2 quarts of water over high heat until it boils. Add the hearts of palm and bring the water back up to a boil. Reduce the heat and simmer for 10 minutes. Remove the hearts of palm from the water and cool to room temperature. Cut off and discard the woody outer layer, then slice them crosswise $1/8$ inch thick. Place the hearts of palm pieces in a bowl and set aside. In a stainless steel saucepan over high heat, bring the pickling liquid to a boil. Pour the boiling liquid over the hearts of palm pieces. Allow them to cool to room temperature before using. The hearts of palm will stay fresh for weeks refrigerated in an airtight container.

CAIPIRINHA

MAKES 1 COCKTAIL

Cachaça is the official spirit of Brazil. If you ever get a chance to visit this lively South American country, you'll discover hundreds of brands of the sugarcane spirit in both aged and unaged varieties. Very little *cachaça* makes its way out of Brazil, but the little that does resembles light rum (not surprisingly, as both liquors are made of the same ingredients) with a more honey-floral quality. Be sure to use ripe limes. If the lime you use isn't very juicy, you may need to add more lime juice to get the right amount of tartness. If you want to use some different citrus fruits in this drink, try muddling in a whole Rangpur lime or half of a Meyer lemon.

1 lime, cut into 8 pieces
1/2 ounce simple syrup (see page 20)
2 ounces cachaça

TOSS the lime pieces into a mixing glass and muddle them down well. Add the simple syrup and *cachaça* and stir well. Add enough ice to fill the mixing glass three-quarters full, cover, and shake a few times. Pour into a short double rocks or old-fashioned glass to serve.

SALTED AND SUGARED RIMS

When citrus fruits are being showcased in drinks, as they are during the winter months at Cyrus, a salted or sugared rim wakes up the palate for the sip to come. People who like a sweet cocktail can work their way around the lip of a sugared glass to get a hit of sweetness with each sip, while people who prefer a tart cocktail can simply drink from the same spot on the rim each time.

Sea salt, which is available in a wide variety of colors, gets its lovely hue from the mineral content of the water from which it is harvested. Black lava and red alaea sea salts from Hawaii are visually stunning and especially tasty on the rim of a fresh margarita when combined with sugar and dried lime zest.

I generally use granulated white sugar on my rims, but I also like the coarse grain and molasses flavor of turbinado (sugar in the raw) for some cocktails. Seek out organic and sustainably manufactured sugars at natural food stores.

You're not limited to salt and sugar when it comes to rims. I pair both of these ingredients with coarsely ground spices and even brightly colored citrus zest for visual appeal and more complex flavor. Feel free to add ground spices, citrus zest, or both to salt and sugar. You might also dry or dehydrate colorful edible flowers, crush or chop the petals, and add these to your salted or sugared rims.

To salt or sugar a rim:

1. Pour a $1/4$-inch layer of salt or sugar onto a flat plate.

2. Cut a lemon or other citrus fruit (or try a blood orange for more color) in half and rub one piece of the citrus around the rim of the glass. Shake off any excess juice.
3. Turn the glass upside down and dip the wet rim into the salt or sugar. Lift the glass straight up and gently shake off any excess.

To add ground spices to a rim:
1. Grind the spices into a coarse powder.
2. Mix five parts salt or sugar to one part spice, then follow steps 1 through 3 above to coat the rim.

To add citrus zest to a rim:
1. Using a microplane grater, zest 2 whole citrus fruits.
2. Using dry paper towels, press out as much of the oil and moisture from the zest as possible (oranges have particularly oily skins). If the zest is still a little bit wet after pressing, place it on a sunny windowsill for an hour or so to dry further.
3. Once the zest is dry, chop it into a coarse powder and follow steps 1 through 3 above to coat the rim.

CLASSIC MARGARITA

MAKES 1 COCKTAIL

It seems a bit odd to be making the national drinks of sunny places like Brazil and Mexico in the wintertime, but in Northern California, this is when the citrus season peaks. These classic refreshers typically include a delicious dose of fresh lime juice, but there's no reason you can't add or substitute other winter citrus juices. Try adding the juice of a blood orange half to the margarita. Whatever you do, please use Cointreau instead of triple sec; they aren't the same thing, and Cointreau makes a big difference in taste. And while this recipe reflects that I like my cocktails tart, you can jack up the amount of simple syrup to your taste.

I'm partial to 100 percent agave silver (*plata*) tequilas from excellent producers like Partida, Don Julio, Chinaco, and El Tesoro. Silver tequila hasn't been barrel aged, so you only taste pure agave flavors in your cocktail. If you like a woody flavor in your margarita, I suggest using a *reposado* tequila; these have been aged in barrels for three to twelve months. *Añejo* tequilas, which are aged for up to five years, are best for sipping, like a fine brandy.

1/2 lime, for rim

3 tablespoons black sea salt, for rim

2 ounces 100 percent agave silver (plata) tequila

1/2 ounce Cointreau

3/4 ounce freshly squeezed lime juice

1/4 ounce simple syrup (see page 20)

RUB the lime half around the rim of a tall collins glass and shake off any excess juice. Dip the glass into the salt to coat the rim (see page 38). Combine the tequila, Cointreau, juice, and syrup in a mixing glass and stir well. Add enough ice to fill the glass, cover, and shake well. Pour into the salt-rimmed glass to serve.

BEACHFIRE MARGARITA

MAKES 1 COCKTAIL

I call this a Beachfire Margarita because the smoky nuances of mescal remind me of a driftwood bonfire on the beach. My favorite mescals are San Luis del Rio, Minero, and Chichicapa, all made under the auspices of Del Maguey. Fans of peaty Islay single-malts will probably enjoy this margarita, too.

$3/4$ ounce 100 percent agave silver (plata) tequila
$3/4$ ounce Del Maguey mescal
$1/2$ ounce Cointreau
$3/4$ ounce freshly squeezed lime juice
$1/4$ ounce simple syrup (see page 20)

COMBINE all of the ingredients in a mixing glass and stir well. Add enough ice to fill the glass, cover, and shake a few times. Pour into a tall collins glass to serve.

Variation: Add salt to the rim. Rub lime around the rim of the tall collins glass and shake off any excess juice. Dip the glass into your choice of salt to coat the rim (see page 38).

FLORES MARGARITA

MAKES 1 COCKTAIL

In late fall, we get pineapple guavas from Cyrus general manger Robert Coffing, who lives in nearby Alexander Valley, and from Henry and Colleen Flores, who live in Healdsburg. These plants grow up to fifteen feet tall and produce both edible flowers in the spring and delicious tropical fruits in the fall. Pineapple guavas can be eaten whole and are also delicious with ice cream. This cocktail is fresh and full of lime flavor like the Classic Margarita, with the added bonus of pineapple, banana, and other tropical notes.

2 ripe pineapple guavas
2 ounces 100 percent agave silver (plata) tequila
1/2 ounce Cointreau
3/4 ounce freshly squeezed lime juice
1/2 ounce simple syrup

SLICE one of the pineapple guavas into quarter-sized medallions and set aside. Cut the other pineapple guava in half lengthwise. With a small spoon, scoop out the flesh and place it in a mixing glass; muddle it down. Add the liquors, juice, and simple syrup, and stir well. Add enough ice to fill the glass, cover, and shake hard a few times. Pour into a tall collins glass and garnish with 3 or 4 pineapple guava medallions to serve.

Variation: Add salt to the rim. Rub lime around the rim of the tall collins glass and shake off any excess juice. Dip the glass into your choice of salt to coat the rim (see page 38).

CHAPTER 2

SPRING

AFTER we are blessed with so much wonderful citrus for the winter months, our local supply inevitably begins to taper off around March. One by one, our citrus sources are depleted, and the unpredictable conditions of springtime mean there's an indeterminate period of time when local farmers don't have much to offer. Because frost is a big threat in Northern California, farmers generally don't plant herbs or edible flowers until at least April for fear that winter may temporarily set in again. This time of year may seem like the most challenging for the seasonally minded bartender, but with a little ingenuity, spring drinks can be some of the most unique and creative of the whole year.

While herbs and flowers are tough to grow in winter if you don't have a greenhouse, farms are able to produce a bounty of winter vegetables. Many of these veggies, including beets, fennel, and numerous varieties of onion, are delicious when pickled. The Cyrus kitchen staff pickles vegetables throughout the year using a versatile and delicious pickling liquid (page 52) that Chef Keane originally picked up from Gray Kunz at Lespinasse. The spiced vinegar flavors in this pickling liquid can make for some interesting nuances in cocktails, whether the liquid itself is an ingredient or pickled vegetables are added to a drink as a garnish.

The variety, color, and fragrance of spring's earliest flowers are one of nature's greatest gifts, as they signify both the end of winter and the birth of new foliage. Many of these flowers are edible and can be used in cuisine and cocktails, so I have provided a list of some of my favorites (see page 129). I tend to use only small flowers with beautiful shapes and colors and a mild flavor or virtually no flavor at all. Flowers in cocktails should complement and echo other ingredients in the glass. For example, I use jasmine blossoms in a drink containing mandarin orange blossom vodka (Plum Dandy; page 99) and borage and dianthus flowers in a cocktail with other early spring ingredients such as fennel fronds and anise hyssop (Frondsong; page 49).

With so little produce coming from the farms, I find that spring is also the perfect time of year to revisit some classic cocktail recipes. The Manhattan, Sazerac, Last Word, and others have stood the test of time because they are winning combinations of classic spirits. Many of these cocktails are composed of mostly straight liquors and a little citrus juice or fresh produce. Because there are so few components, every ingredient must be measured accurately and only carefully selected spirits should be used. If you overpour or underpour any ingredient, the drink will taste dramatically different. I have suggested specific brands for each of the classic cocktail recipes. Feel free to experiment with other brands, but give my recommendations a shot, too. All gins are not the same, nor are all bourbons or brandies—and I chose the ones used in these recipes because I think they make the best cocktail.

SPRING GIN COCKTAILS

Although the legal definition of gin is "a neutral grain spirit whose primary flavoring is juniper berry," almost all gins incorporate myriad other dried and sometimes fresh botanicals. These additional ingredients give individual gins their distinctive flavors and aromatic profiles. Because of the botanically enhanced backbone of most gins, I've found that they pair well with pickled vegetables and fresh herbs. Sarticious gin is small-batch gin made in Santa Cruz, California, that incorporates numerous dried and fresh herbs, including cilantro. Naturally, this gin matches very well with drinks that feature fresh herbs, and it is the obvious choice for drinks featuring citrus and pickled veggies.

APRIL SHOWER

MAKES 1 COCKTAIL

> The fresh flavors of spring onion, flat-leaf parsley, verjuice (unripe grape juice), lemon, and gin combine to deliver a tart and refreshing cooler tied together with a complex layer of pickling liquid. I call this an April Shower because most of the ingredients show up in April and every part of this drink tastes fresh and clean.

10 flat-leaf (Italian) parsley leaves

1 1/2 ounces Sarticious gin

1/2 ounce white verjuice (see page 90)

1/4 ounce Ultimate Pickling Liquid (page 52)

3/4 ounce freshly squeezed lemon juice

1/2 ounce simple syrup (see page 20)

1 spring onion, white part only, cut into thin rings

10 Pickled Pearl Onions (page 53)

PLACE the parsley leaves in a mixing glass and tap a few times with a muddler to release their flavor. Add the gin, verjuice, pickling liquid, juice, and syrup and give it a stir. Add the onions and enough ice to fill the glass. Cover and shake a few times. Pour into a tall collins glass to serve.

FRONDSONG

MAKES 1 COCKTAIL

Fans of anise or licorice will love this cocktail because the flavor is woven into this tart drink in many forms. Pickled fennel, Green Chartreuse, fresh anise hyssop, and a pastis from New Orleans called Herbsaint just sing when added to gin, lemon juice, and sugar. When you pour this cocktail into the glass around a fennel frond, you let the world know there's a lot of licorice in the drink. Be sure to choose a frond that's just slightly taller than the glass so it sticks out the top. I love to garnish this drink with dianthus and borage flowers because they are two of the first edible flowers we get from Love Farms every spring.

1 1/2 ounces Sarticious gin

1/4 ounce Herbsaint or other pastis

1/4 ounce Green Chartreuse

3/4 ounce freshly squeezed lemon juice

1/2 ounce simple syrup (see page 20)

5 pieces Pickled Fennel (page 53)

5 anise hyssop leaves, cut into chiffonade

1 fennel frond, for garnish

2 or 3 dianthus flowers, for garnish (optional)

2 or 3 borage flowers, for garnish (optional)

COMBINE the gin, Herbsaint, Green Chartreuse, juice, and simple syrup in a mixing glass and give it a stir. Add the fennel pieces, anise hyssop leaves, and enough ice to fill the mixing glass. Cover and shake a few times. Pinch the top of the fennel frond and lower it into a stemmed water glass or a tall collins glass. While still pinching the top of the frond, pour the drink around the frond and into the glass. Remove the petals from the dianthus flowers and place them and the borage flowers atop the drink. Use a straw or a knife to push the flowers down into the drink so they're evenly dispersed.

GIN KIMCHI

MAKES 1 COCKTAIL

Kimchi (pickled and fermented vegetables served with Korean food) has always scared me. The flavor can be intensely pungent and the texture rather slippery. Some of the cooks in the Cyrus kitchen were pickling radishes one day, and the smell caught me off guard. At first I thought they were making kimchi, but they explained that pickled radishes, while not a true kimchi, throw off an intense smell reminiscent of fermented vegetation. While the radishes smelled almost offensive, they tasted delicious. I wondered if the strong aroma and flavor might work well in a cocktail in the same way that musk is a nice undertone in cologne. This was the tasty result.

1 1/2 ounces Sarticious gin

3/4 ounce freshly squeezed lemon juice

1/2 ounce Ginger-Shiso Syrup (see recipe)

8 pieces Pickled Ginger (page 54)

8 pieces Pickled Daikon (page 52)

5 small shiso leaves, cut into chiffonade

3/4 ounce Bundaberg or Cock'n Bull ginger beer

COMBINE the gin, juice, and syrup in a mixing glass and give it a stir. Add the pickled vegetables, the shiso, and enough ice to fill the mixing glass. Cover and shake a few times. Add the ginger beer, and pour it into a stemmed water glass or a tall collins glass to serve.

Ginger-Shiso Syrup

MAKES 1 CUP (ENOUGH FOR ABOUT 16 COCKTAILS)

1 cup simple syrup, chilled (see page 20)

2 drops essential oil of ginger

2 drops essential oil of galangal

1 drop essential oil of perilla (shiso)

COMBINE the simple syrup and essential oils in an airtight container. Cover and shake well to mix the oils into the syrup. The simple syrup will keep for about 2 weeks refrigerated in the airtight container.

ULTIMATE PICKLING LIQUID

This recipe makes enough pickling liquid to last quite a while, but it also keeps well for up to 6 months if stored in an airtight container in the refrigerator. If you want to make a smaller amount, scale the recipe down by one-fourth or one-half. You can blanch your vegetables before pickling to make them softer, but I happen to like my pickled treats as crunchy as possible.

MAKES 1 GALLON

8 teaspoons fennel seeds

3 tablespoons dill seeds

5 teaspoons fenugreek

$1/4$ cup coriander seeds

$5^3/4$ cups sugar

11 cups white wine vinegar

6 cloves

2 large or 3 small bay leaves

$2^1/2$ (3-inch) cinnamon sticks

4 dried Hunan chiles

Heat a stainless steel sauté pan over medium heat and follow the instructions on page 20 to toast the whole fennel, dill, fenugreek, and coriander seeds until aromatic (do *not* grind down the spices before or after toasting). Remove from the heat and set aside.

Combine the sugar and vinegar in a large stainless steel stockpot over high heat and bring the mixture to a boil. Stir in the toasted seeds and the cloves, bay leaves, cinnamon sticks, and chiles, then remove the stockpot from the heat. Allow the liquid to cool before pouring into airtight containers.

Pickled Fennel

The licorice notes of fennel blend well with the dill and fennel seeds in our pickling liquid. Try this in the Frondsong (page 49), which continues the theme by using anise hyssop and pastis (aniseed liqueur). Pickled fennel is also wonderful on green salads and beet salads.

MAKES 40 TO 60 PIECES (ENOUGH FOR 8 TO 12 COCKTAILS)

2 fennel bulbs

1 quart Ultimate Pickling Liquid (see recipe)

Cut the fennel bulbs into ¹/₈-inch-thick slices using a mandoline and place in an airtight container. Reserve the fronds and discard any unsightly pieces. In a stainless steel saucepan over high heat, bring 1 quart of water to a boil, then pour it over the fennel to blanch. Drain the water from the container and place the fennel back into the container. In the same saucepan over high heat, bring the pickling liquid to a boil, then pour it over the blanched fennel. Place the container, uncovered, in the refrigerator to cool. The fennel will keep for up to 1 week refrigerated and covered in the airtight container.

Pickled Pearl Onions

If you like onions in your martinis, these pickled pearls are the ultimate treat. And they are really the best garnish for a Gibson that I've ever had.

MAKES 100 PEARL ONIONS (ENOUGH FOR ABOUT 10 COCKTAILS)

  100 white or purple pearl onions

  4 cups Ultimate Pickling Liquid (see recipe)

Remove the dry outer skins from the onions and discard. Place the onions in an airtight container and set aside. In a large stainless steel saucepan over high heat, bring the pickling liquid to a boil. Pour it over the onions and let cool to at least room temperature before using. They will keep for months refrigerated in the airtight container.

Asian Pickling Liquid

I created a different pickling liquid, made from mirin, sake, and rice wine vinegar, for ginger and daikon because the Asian ingredients work well together.

MAKES 1²/₃ CUPS

  1 cup rice wine vinegar

  ¹/₃ cup mirin

  ¹/₃ cup filtered sake

  ¹/₂ cup sugar

Combine the rice wine vinegar, mirin, and sake in a stainless steel saucepan over high heat. Bring the mixture to a boil, add the sugar, and stir until it dissolves. Allow the liquid to cool before pouring into an airtight container.

ULTIMATE PICKLING LIQUID, continued

Pickled Ginger

Adding a cooked red beet to the liquid will stain the ginger, making it look like the pink ginger often served with sushi, but this step is optional.

MAKES 40 TO 60 PIECES (ENOUGH FOR 5 TO 8 COCKTAILS)

$1/2$ pound ginger, peeled and sliced into $1/8$-inch pieces

$1^2/_3$ cups Asian Pickling Liquid (see page 53)

1 small red beet, cooked and peeled (optional)

In a large saucepan over high heat, bring 1 quart of water to a boil. Place the ginger pieces in an airtight container and pour the boiling water over the ginger. Let it rest for 5 minutes, then drain out the water and place the ginger back into the container. In a stainless steel saucepan over high heat, bring the pickling liquid to a boil. Remove the saucepan from the heat and pour the liquid over the blanched ginger pieces, then cut the beet into about 5 slices and add it. Place the container, uncovered, in the refrigerator to cool. The beet will bleed a deep reddish color to turn the ginger pieces pink in about 24 hours. Remove the beet when the ginger achieves a nice pink color. The ginger will keep for up to 3 weeks refrigerated and covered in the airtight container.

Pickled Daikon

Pickled radishes smell really funky, but don't let the aroma scare you. They actually do taste quite good. Try them in the Gin Kimchi (page 51).

MAKES 40 TO 60 SLICES (ENOUGH FOR 8 TO 12 COCKTAILS)

1 (10-inch) daikon, peeled and thinly sliced

1 quart Asian Pickling Liquid (see page 53)

Place the daikon pieces in an airtight container. In a stainless steel saucepan over high heat, bring the pickling liquid to a boil and pour it over the daikon pieces. Place the container, uncovered, in the refrigerator to cool. The daikon will keep for up to 1 week refrigerated and covered in the airtight container.

CUBA LIBRE

MAKES 1 COCKTAIL

The origins of this cocktail go back to the Spanish-American War, but it became really popular after the Andrews Sisters' song in the mid-1940s. The Cuba Libre is a simple drink meant for the masses. Be gentle when you stir it so you don't ruin the fizz of the Coca-Cola.

2 ounces Charbay cane rum

3 ounces Mexican Coca-Cola, chilled (see page 60)

¼ ounce freshly squeezed lime juice

Perfect ice cubes (see page 58)

COMBINE the rum, cola, and juice in a mixing glass and stir gently. Fill a tall collins glass with the ice cubes and pour the drink over the ice to serve.

GIN AND TONIC

MAKES 1 COCKTAIL

British officers serving in India and elsewhere during the nineteenth century drank tonic water made with quinine to fend off malaria. Adding a little gin to the water made the bitter-tasting tonic easier to drink and it also gave them a buzz. Since then, the gin and tonic has become one of the world's most beloved cocktails. I know that gin drinkers can be very brand loyal, but I would invite them to be as devoted to their choice of tonic water. No one at Fever-Tree (or anyone else, for that matter) has ever paid me to endorse the product, so you can rest assured I really mean it when I say this tonic water rises far above the rest.

Perfect ice cubes (see page 58)
1 juicy lime wedge
1¹/₂ ounces Junípero gin, or your favorite brand
2 ounces Fever-Tree tonic water, chilled

FILL a short (8-ounce) old-fashioned glass with the ice cubes. Squeeze the lime wedge over the ice and drop it into the glass. Add the gin and then the tonic water. Stir gently and serve.

PERFECT ICE CUBES

I'm the first to admit that I take my cocktails seriously, but even I am not about to buy a Kold-Draft machine (with a retail price of $3,000 to $6,000) to make perfect, dense cubes of ice at home. You can actually make similar ice cubes at home with distilled or filtered water and silicone ice cube trays. These flexible and inexpensive trays turn out perfectly square ice cubes that will keep your drink colder longer. They melt more slowly than store-bought ice because there is less surface area in contact with the liquid. Be sure to cover your trays tightly with plastic wrap before you put them in the freezer so your cubes don't take on the flavor of the frozen food they might be sitting next to. Die-hard gin and tonic fans can even freeze their tonic water in these trays so their drinks don't get watered down.

DARK AND STORMY

MAKES 1 COCKTAIL

A purist would insist that you use Gosling's Black Seal rum to make this drink, but I've found that this particular variation on the national drink of Bermuda is even better. Be gentle when you stir this drink so you don't ruin the fizz of the ginger beer.

2 ounces Charbay cane rum

3 ounces Bundaberg or Cock'n Bull ginger
   beer, chilled

¼ ounce freshly squeezed lime juice

1 dash Angostura bitters

Perfect ice cubes (see page 58)

COMBINE the rum, ginger beer, juice, and bitters in a mixing glass and stir gently. Fill a tall collins glass with the ice and pour the drink over the ice to serve.

SODAS AND MIXERS

Artificially flavored, mass-produced sodas and mixers sweetened with high-fructose corn syrup make poor quality cocktails—period. Even simple classic combinations like a rum and coke or a gin and tonic can taste extraordinary if quality mixers and spirits are used. Many of the products listed below have very little sugar, making them perfect for pairing with food for people who don't drink alcohol. Always refrigerate your mixers so they aren't too warm, which causes the ice to melt too fast and dilute the drink. Many of these brands are widely available. Otherwise, a quick search on the Internet will guide you to a retailer near you.

Bundaberg ginger beer: This is my favorite ginger beer. It's sweet and made with real sugar. Cock'n Bull is a good second choice, but it contains high-fructose corn syrup.

Citrus juice: Always, always, always squeeze your own fresh citrus juice, strain it, and then keep it refrigerated. Be sure to use it within 48 hours for peak flavor and freshness (see page 10).

Cranberry juice: Whether you drink this on its own or as a mixer, 100 percent unsweetened cranberry juice gives you better color and more tannin than the sweetened juice or cranberry juice cocktails. Read the label; the ingredients panel should list nothing other than cranberry juice. Although the unsweetened juice is virtually undrinkable on its own, just add simple syrup to it, $1/4$ cup at a time, until you find the right sweetness level. Regardless of how much sweetener you add, the color will remain deep red.

Dry Soda: This company uses essential oils and cane sugar to make lemongrass, lavender, rhubarb, and kumquat sodas. They are absolutely delicious, are great for food pairings, and work well with rums, vodkas, and flavored vodkas.

Fever-Tree: Fever-Tree's tonic water, bitter lemon, and ginger ale are second to none. They are made with real cane sugar (and very little of it) as well as real quinine, essential oils, and other ingredients.

Mexican Coca-Cola: This south-of-the-border version of American Coca-Cola has a slightly different formulation, and thus no high-fructose corn syrup (plus, it comes in the classic glass bottle). Serve it ice cold with no ice and you'll realize how good this beverage can be.

Nana Mae's Organics: This Sonoma County company makes high-quality pear and apple juices (including from heirloom apples), as well as a lemonade using Meyer lemons. At Cyrus, we mix them in cocktails and also serve them on their own.

Navarro Vineyards: This Anderson Valley winery releases unfermented Pinot Noir and Gewürztraminer juice every year; both are stellar.

Seltzer Sisters: This company sells pure water that comes in attractive bottles charged with carbon dioxide. It is available only in the Bay Area. If you can't find this seltzer, use the 10-ounce soda bottles from Schweppes or Canada Dry.

Sonoma Sparkler: This local Sonoma County company produces excellent sparkling juice-based beverages using apples, pears, peaches, and raspberries, as well as a sparkling lemonade. At Cyrus, we mix them in cocktails and also serve them on their own.

Sweet and sour mix: If you take one thing away from this book, I hope it is that you should never buy commercial sweet and sour mix again. It is so simple to make yourself. Just combine one part fresh lemon juice, one part fresh lime juice, and one part simple syrup. It's so easy, and it really does make much better drinks.

MARIPOSA AVIATION

MAKES 1 COCKTAIL (see photo on page 66)

The aviation cocktail first appeared just before Prohibition, but really took flight during the days of Charles Lindbergh and Amelia Earhart. It is a simple but perfect medley of three ingredients: gin, maraschino liqueur, and freshly squeezed lemon juice. I prefer the heavy juniper flavor of Anchor Distillery's Junipero gin for this cocktail, but feel free to use any dry style of gin. The combination of tart lemon juice, the sweet and floral liqueur, and juniper makes this a well-balanced cocktail that soars acrosss the palate.

2 ounces Junípero gin
1/2 ounce Luxardo maraschino liqueur
3/4 ounce freshly squeezed lemon juice
1 Amarena cherry, for garnish

PLACE a V-shaped glass in the freezer to chill.

Combine the gin, liqueur, and juice in a mixing glass and stir well. Add enough ice to fill the mixing glass, cover, and shake hard for 7 seconds. Strain into the chilled glass and drop the Amarena cherry into the glass to serve.

RUDD NEGRONI

MAKES 1 COCKTAIL (see photo on page 68)

The Negroni is a classic Italian cocktail named for a count from Florence who was looking for a variation on an Americano. This complex and delicious drink with herb, citrus, and fortified red wine nuances has recently experienced a well-deserved resurgence in popularity. I prefer to zest an orange over my Negroni, but traditional recipes call for a lemon instead. Every gin is different, but give Leslie Rudd's 209, made in San Francisco, a try. I love it in this cocktail.

1 1/2 ounces 209 gin

1 ounce Carpano Antica or other Italian-style
   sweet vermouth

1 ounce Campari

1 orange, unwaxed and scrubbed

PLACE a short rocks glass or a V-shaped glass in the freezer to chill.

Combine the gin, vermouth, and Campari in a mixing glass and stir well. Add enough ice to fill the mixing glass and stir for 15 seconds. Strain the drink into the chilled glass and, using a zester, zest the orange over the drink so the oils spray into the glass. Twist the zest into a cork-screw and drop it into the drink.

From left to right: Frankfort Manhattan and Bourbon Infused with Vanilla and Citrus Peel (page 72).

FRANKFORT MANHATTAN

MAKES 1 COCKTAIL

This cocktail was born in Manhattan (supposedly at the Manhattan Hotel) in the 1870s and has been a staple of the American cocktail repertoire ever since. Our Frankfort Manhattan, made with citrus peel and vanilla bean infused twelve-year-old Weller bourbon (made in Frankfort, Kentucky), sweet vermouth, and Angostura bitters, is served year-round at Cyrus. I always garnish this cocktail with two Amarena (never maraschino) cherries (see page 121).

2$\frac{1}{4}$ ounces Bourbon Infused with Vanilla and Citrus Peel (page 72)

$\frac{3}{4}$ ounce Noilly Prat sweet vermouth

3 dashes Angostura bitters

2 Amarena cherries, for garnish

PLACE a V-shaped glass in the freezer to chill.

Combine the bourbon, sweet vermouth, and bitters in a mixing glass and stir well. Add enough ice to fill the mixing glass three-quarters full and stir for 15 seconds more. Strain into the chilled glass and garnish with two Amarena cherries skewered on a pick.

Clockwise from top: The Last Word (page 71),
Mendo Sidecar, and Mariposa Aviation (page 62).

MENDO SIDECAR

MAKES 1 COCKTAIL

First created during World War I in either London or Paris, this Cognac-based cocktail traditionally had only two other ingredients, Cointreau and lemon juice. I've discovered that Germain-Robin XO brandy, made with a high percentage of Pinot Noir grapes, is a fantastic base for a sidecar, but you can also use VSOP Cognac or another well-aged brandy. The maraschino liqueur adds a lovely floral high note. Spraying the drink with orange oil gives you a fresh citrus aroma as you start to take a sip. Most sidecars are served in a sugar-rimmed glass, but I don't feel that this version needs it.

1 1/2 ounces Germain-Robin XO brandy
1/2 ounce Cointreau
1/4 ounce Luxardo maraschino liqueur
3/4 ounce freshly squeezed lemon juice
1 orange, unwaxed and scrubbed

PLACE a V-shaped glass in the freezer to chill.

Combine the brandy, Cointreau, liqueur, and juice in a mixing glass and stir well. Add enough ice to fill the mixing glass, cover, and shake hard for 7 seconds. Strain the drink into the chilled glass and, using a zester, zest the orange over the drink so the oils spray into the glass. Twist the zest into a corkscrew and drop it into the drink.

From left to right: Rudd Negroni (page 63) and Handy Sazerac.

HANDY SAZERAC

MAKES 1 COCKTAIL

Many cocktail historians consider the Sazerac to be America's first cocktail. It was originally made with Cognac until a little pest called *Phylloxera* ruined French grape crops in the later part of the nineteenth century. After that, bartenders turned to American-made rye whiskey and never looked back. Traditionally, only Peychaud's bitters, an anise-driven variety made in New Orleans, would be used in this drink, but I like to add a few dashes of Angostura bitters, which has a cardamom-spice flavor, for depth and complexity. Thomas H. Handy rye is over 130 proof, meaning the dilution that occurs during stirring will render a somewhat mellow cocktail with a spicy bite and long finish. Zesting a lemon over the top of this drink adds fresh citrus oils; you can either drop the zest into the drink or discard it.

$1/4$ ounce Herbsaint, absinthe, or other pastis

1 white sugar cube

3 dashes Angostura bitters

3 dashes Peychaud's bitters

2 ounces Thomas H. Handy rye whiskey

1 lemon, unwaxed and scrubbed

PLACE a short rocks or old-fashioned glass in the freezer to chill.

Add the Herbsaint to the chilled glass, swirl it around to give the inside of the glass a thin coating, and then discard the excess.

Place the sugar cube in the bottom of a mixing glass and douse it with the bitters. Muddle down the sugar and add the rye whiskey. Stir well, until the sugar is mostly dissolved. Add enough ice to fill the mixing glass three-quarters full and stir for about 15 seconds. Strain the drink into the coated glass and, using a potato peeler or a sharp pairing knife, zest the lemon over the top. Drop the zest into the drink or discard it.

PAPPY OLD-FASHIONED

MAKES 1 COCKTAIL

There are very few bourbons available that are fifteen years old or older. The Van Winkle family releases a small amount of fifteen-, twenty-, and twenty-three-year-old bottles every year. If you ever see any of these on a store shelf, buy any and all of them. Besides being delicious on their own, they make wonderful cocktails, particularly this take on a classic old-fashioned.

1 sugar cube

2 dashes Angostura bitters

2 dashes orange bitters

$1/2$ orange slice

3 Amarena cherries, for garnish

$1/2$ ounce seltzer

2 ounces Pappy Van Winkle's 15-year-old bourbon

PLACE the sugar cube in the bottom of a mixing glass and douse it with the bitters. Toss in the orange slice, one of the cherries, and the seltzer, and muddle it down. Add the bourbon and stir well. Add enough ice to fill the mixing glass half full and stir a few times to mix. Pour the drink into a short (7- to 8-ounce) old-fashioned glass to serve. Garnish with remaining 2 Amarena cherries skewered on a pick.

THE LAST WORD

MAKES 1 COCKTAIL (see photo on page 66)

This cocktail first appeared during Prohibition. The gin is made with about a dozen botanicals and the Chartreuse with more than a hundred. The floral cherry notes of maraschino liqueur work perfectly with all of the ingredients, and the tartness of fresh lime juice makes this classic refreshing as well. This drink seems to have it all, which is why it might be my favorite of all time.

3/4 ounce Green Chartreuse

3/4 ounce Plymouth or London Dry–style gin

3/4 ounce Luxardo maraschino liqueur

3/4 ounce freshly squeezed lime juice

1 Amarena cherry, for garnish

PLACE a V-shaped glass in the freezer to chill.

Combine the Chartreuse, gin, liqueur, and juice in a mixing glass and stir well. Add enough ice to fill the mixing glass three-quarters full, cover, and shake hard for 7 seconds. Strain the drink into the chilled glass and drop in the cherry to serve.

BOURBON INFUSED WITH VANILLA AND CITRUS PEEL

MAKES 1 (1-LITER) BOTTLE (see photo on page 64)

At Cyrus, we make this bourbon infusion by the case, but you can make it by the bottle just as easily. The key is to use a container that is large enough to hold all of the bourbon and catch the oil spray of the citrus zest. The combination of well-aged bourbon with notes of caramel and vanilla, sweet and smoky vanilla pods, and fresh citrus zest produces a sipping bourbon or a wonderful addition to classic whiskey cocktails. Like cellos (see page 12), infused bourbon makes a great holiday gift. Note that it takes at least a week for the bourbon to fully infuse.

1 (1-liter) bottle W. L. Weller 12-year-old bourbon, or other well-aged bourbon

1 orange, unwaxed and scrubbed

1 lemon, unwaxed and scrubbed

1 vanilla bean

POUR the bourbon into a large airtight container. Using a $1/4$-inch-wide zester, zest the orange and lemon over and into the container. Avoid the bitter white pith as much as possible and try to make long, shoestring-like zests. Split the vanilla bean pod lengthwise and turn it inside out. Don't remove the seeds. Add the vanilla pod to the bourbon. Close the container and store it in a dark, cook place. Stir the bourbon mixture once per day for a week to mix the ingredients. After 1 week, carefully pour the infused bourbon back into the bottle. Add 1 strip each of the orange and lemon zests and the vanilla bean, then seal up the bottle.

STAINING

Rather than using artificial food coloring to give our drinks and edible parts a beautiful hue, I like to stain my drinks naturally. To do this, I boil simple syrup and then steep brightly colored foods in the syrup for as long as it takes to color the liquid. Using this same technique, it's possible to stain juices, purees, and pickling liquids. Any fruits or vegetables that you immerse in the colored liquid will take on its color eventually, giving you countless possibilities for embellishing your cocktails in adventurous ways. When you use certain natural, organic ingredients for color, they don't affect the flavor of the syrup very much, and therefore don't adversely affect the flavor of your drinks, either. There's a rainbow of potential colors; here are my favorites:

Red: pomegranate juice or red beet (to achieve pink, reduce the steeping time)

Orange: orange beet

Yellow: yellow beet or fresh turmeric root

Green: combine the staining agents for yellow and blue; I've had some success with cooked spinach, but it takes a lot of leaves

Blue: red carrot or blueberry

Purple: red grape juice or blackberries

Black: squid ink (ask your fishmonger)

From left to right: Beau Regards (page 76) and Rhubarbarella.

RHUBARBARELLA

MAKES 1 COCKTAIL

The Rhubarbarella and the Beau Regards (page 76) are essentially the same drink with one ingredient changed. I serve the Rhubarbarella in late spring, when rhubarb first appears, then switch to the Beau Regards in early summer to take advantage of the season's first plump blueberries. The tart bite of the rhubarb is tempered by steeping it in a red beet–stained simple syrup enhanced with essences of ginger, galangal, and shiso.

$3/4$ ounce Hangar One Buddha's hand vodka

$3/4$ ounce vodka

$3/4$ ounce freshly squeezed lemon juice

$1/2$ ounce Rhubarbarella Simple Syrup
(see recipe)

$3/4$ ounce seltzer

10 pieces Candied Rhubarb (see recipe)

5 shiso leaves, cut into chiffonade

COMBINE the vodkas, juice, simple syrup, and seltzer in a mixing glass and give it a stir. Add the rhubarb, shiso, and enough ice to fill the mixing glass. Cover and shake a few times. Pour into a short or tall collins glass to serve and use a straw or knife to evenly distribute the rhubarb pieces and shiso throughout the drink.

Candied Rhubarb and Rhubarbarella Syrup

MAKES $2^2/3$ CUPS SYRUP AND 100 RHUBARB PIECES (ENOUGH FOR ABOUT 10 COCKTAILS)

$2^2/3$ cups simple syrup, chilled
(see page 20)

6 drops essential oil of ginger

6 drops essential oil of galangal

2 drops essential oil of perilla (shiso)

1 small red beet, cooked and peeled

2 medium stalks rhubarb

Combine the simple syrup and essential oils in an airtight container. Cover and shake well. Cut the beet into several slices and add it to the syrup. Cut the ends off the rhubarb so the stalks are

continued

a uniform length, then chop into $^1/_4$-inch pieces. Add the rhubarb to the simple syrup mixture and gently stir. Place the container in the refrigerator and stir a few more times over the next 24 hours so the beets bleed their color evenly. Once the color is red enough, remove and discard the beets. The candied rhubarb pieces and the simple syrup will keep for about 7 days refrigerated.

BEAU REGARDS

MAKES 1 COCKTAIL (see photo on page 74)

The Beau Regards and the Rhubarbarella (page 75) are essentially the same cocktail with one ingredient changed. I serve the Rhubarbarella in late spring, when rhubarb first appears, then switch to the Beau Regards in early summer to take advantage of the season's first plump blueberries. When blueberries start to ripen, I stain the simple syrup with the berries. Both drinks have lots of edible parts, including threads of fresh shiso.

$^3/_4$ ounce Hangar One Buddha's hand vodka

$^3/_4$ ounce vodka

$^1/_2$ ounce Beau Regards Simple Syrup (see recipe)

$^3/_4$ ounce freshly squeezed lemon juice

$^3/_4$ ounce seltzer

5 shiso leaves, cut into chiffonade

10 to 15 fresh blueberries

COMBINE the vodkas, simple syrup, juice, and seltzer in a mixing glass and give it a stir. Add the shiso, blueberries, and enough ice to fill the mixing glass. Cover and shake a few times. Pour into a short bucket glass or tall collins glass to serve and use a straw or knife to evenly distribute the shiso and blueberries throughout the drink.

Beau Regards Simple Syrup

....

MAKES 2 CUPS (ENOUGH FOR ABOUT 32 COCKTAILS)

 2 2/3 cups simple syrup (see page 20)

 1/3 cup fresh blueberries

 6 drops essential oil of ginger

 6 drops essential oil of galangal

 2 drops essential oil of perilla (shiso)

In a large saucepan set over medium-high heat, bring the simple syrup to a boil. Add the blueberries and bring the syrup back to a boil. Reduce the heat to low and simmer for 10 minutes, until the syrup has a blue-purple color. Strain the syrup through a fine-mesh strainer or chinois into an airtight container, and allow it to cool to at least room temperature. Add the essential oils, close the container, and shake well to combine the oils and syrup. The syrup will keep for 2 to 3 weeks refrigerated in the airtight container.

CHAPTER 3

SUMMER

DESPITE the surprising versatility of pickled vegetables and the satisfaction of working with the classics, each spring I eagerly anticipate summer's rich bounty. Healdsburg's two weekly farmers' markets open in May. If we've had a long winter, the pickings may be pretty sparse during the first few weeks. But if we've had an early spring, the May farmers' markets could look like an early summer market in full swing. with fresh herbs, ripe cherries, and an array of delicate summer flowers.

As the warm summer days get longer, dozens of varieties of peaches appear—yellow, white, and even red. That's when the Westside Bellini (page 95)—made from several varieties of white peaches—goes back on the menu. Sebastopol Berry Farm and Ridgeview Farms start selling olallieberries, marionberries, blackberries, and raspberries around this time, too. I buy berries from these farmers until the wild blackberries that grow in the creeks around Healdsburg are ripe for picking. Toward the end of summer, quirky little cucumbers, hundreds of varieties of heirloom tomatoes, and beautiful melons in a rainbow of colors ripen, all of which we use in our fresh cocktails.

I tend to serve more cocktails in tall collins glasses during the summer because. when it's hot outside, people want refreshing drinks served over ice. Although strained cocktails served in a V-shaped glass are festive and colorful, they warm up quickly in the warm air. During this time of year, I also add an abundance of small, edible ingredients like sliced cucumbers, fresh berries, and cherry tomatoes, which gives guests something to munch on while they drink. We even designed a special stainless steel straw with prongs on the end to make fishing out these treats easier. Half straw and half fork, we call it a "stork." (To buy storks for your own bar, order online from www.paulkimura.com.)

During this plentiful season, I have access to far more produce than I could ever possibly use for our small cocktail program. However, if you happen to visit the bar on a warm summer night, you'll see that I do my best to take advantage of everything Northern California's rich agricultural land has to offer.

WHAT IS GINGER BEER?

The first ginger beers, which appeared in Britain in the 1700s, packed a strong ginger flavor and alcoholic punch. Today's ginger beers, made in countries around the world, are generally still fermented but bottled as sodas without the alcohol. Believe it or not, the current vodka craze has its roots in ginger beer.

In the 1950s, Jack Morgan, owner of the Cock'n Bull restaurant on Los Angeles's fabled Sunset Strip, made ginger beer as a side project. However, it wasn't selling well until Jack tried mixing it with Smirnoff vodka and a little lime juice. Because drinking anything Russian-made during the height of the McCarthy era could land you in front of a congressional committee, Jack had to explain that Smirnoff was now an American brand made from American grain. His Moscow Mule cocktail was a hit, and vodka continued to gain in popularity through the '50s and late '60s, when James Bond ordered his vodka martinis shaken and never stirred.

Today, ginger beer is basically an intensely flavored ginger ale. Each brand of ginger beer has a slightly different flavor. I prefer two brands: Cock'n Bull, made domestically, and Bundaberg, from Australia. Ginger beers that are sharply flavored, like Reed's, are wonderful on their own, but can dominate when mixed into cocktails.

THAI BOXER

MAKES 1 COCKTAIL (see photo on page 82)

The foundations of this cocktail include Tahitian vanilla bean–enhanced rum and a Thai trinity of herbs: Thai basil, cilantro, and spearmint (also known commonly as mint). A healthy dose of freshly squeezed lime juice contributes a refreshing tang, and a touch of Thai coconut milk adds welcome richness. Ginger beer rounds everything out with a little fizz.

$1^1/_2$ ounces Charbay Tahitian vanilla rum

$^3/_4$ ounce freshly squeezed lime juice

$^1/_2$ ounce simple syrup (see page 20)

$^1/_2$ ounce Thai coconut milk

$^3/_4$ ounce Bundaberg or Cock'n Bull ginger beer

5 large or 10 small Thai basil leaves, cut into chiffonade

10 spearmint leaves, cut into chiffonade

10 cilantro leaves

1 Thai or purple basil blossom, for garnish

1 bamboo sprig, for garnish

COMBINE the rum, juice, simple syrup, coconut milk, and ginger beer in a mixing glass and stir well. Add the herbs and enough ice to fill the mixing glass, cover, and shake a few times. Pour into a tall collins glass and garnish with the basil blossom and bamboo sprig to serve.

From left to right: Thai Boxer (page 81) and Sunny and Dry.

SUNNY AND DRY

MAKES 1 COCKTAIL

On a hot day, this is about the most refreshing drink you can put to your lips. Although many people are scared of gin, I can honestly tell you that not one vodka drinker has ever sent this drink back (after all, gin is nothing more than a flavored vodka). The herbaceous notes of the gin are accented with lemon verbena, spearmint, and cucumber, and the yellow petals from sunflowers or black-eyed Susans make this cocktail decidedly sunny. While you could use fresh slices of cucumber (I really like striped Armenians) in this cocktail, the extra step of soaking them in a minted simple syrup turns the cukes into deliciously sweet and crunchy bites in an otherwise tart and refreshing cocktail.

5 lemon verbena leaves

2 ounces Sarticious gin

3/4 ounce freshly squeezed lemon juice

1/2 ounce Mint Simple Syrup (see recipe)

3/4 ounce seltzer

10 spearmint leaves, cut into chiffonade

5 to 10 sunflower or black-eyed Susan petals, cut into chiffonade

10 pieces Preserved Cucumber (see recipe)

PLACE the lemon verbena leaves in a mixing glass and tap firmly a few times with a muddler. Add the gin, juice, simple syrup, and seltzer, and stir well. Add the spearmint, flower petals, cucumber, and enough ice to fill the mixing glass. Cover and shake a few times. Pour into a tall collins glass to serve. Use a straw or knife to distribute the ingredients evenly throughout the drink.

continued

Mint Simple Syrup with Preserved Cucumber

....

MAKES 2²/₃ CUPS SYRUP AND ABOUT 100 CUCUMBER PIECES
(ENOUGH FOR ABOUT 10 COCKTAILS)

2²/₃ cups simple syrup, chilled (see page 20)

3 drops essential oil of spearmint

1 thick English or Armenian cucumber, or 2 skinny Armenian cucumbers

Combine the simple syrup and essential oil in an airtight container and shake well. Cut the cucumber in half lengthwise, scoop out the seeds with a small spoon, and chop the cucumber into ¹/₄-inch pieces. Add the cucumber pieces to the syrup mixture and allow them to marinate for 15 minutes before using. The cucumbers will begin to get flabby after about 2 days, so use them right away. You can continue to use the simple syrup for another day or so, but when the cucumbers make the syrup smell a bit off, discard it.

MINT JULEP

MAKES 1 COCKTAIL

I've been told that there are as many mint julep recipes in Kentucky as there are blades of blue-grass, but they all have one thing in common: a good-quality mint-flavored simple syrup. You can make a minted simple syrup by steeping lots of fresh spearmint in simple syrup for twenty-four hours, or you can do what I do and infuse simple syrup with essential oil of spearmint (see page 84; simply eliminate the cucumbers). Mint juleps are traditionally served with crushed ice in a silver or pewter cup, but at Cyrus I prefer to serve them in a chilled old-fashioned glass.

2 ounces Kentucky straight bourbon whiskey

10 spearmint leaves, cut into chiffonade

$^1/_2$ ounce Mint Simple Syrup (page 84)

Spearmint sprig, for garnish

PLACE an old-fashioned glass filled with crushed ice in the freezer to chill.

Combine the whiskey, spearmint, and simple syrup in a mixing glass and stir. Add enough ice to fill the mixing glass and shake vigorously for 5 seconds. Strain over the crushed ice in the chilled glass and garnish with a spearmint sprig.

MOJITO

MAKES 1 COCKTAIL

A mojito's basic components are rum, freshly squeezed lime juice, sugar, and spearmint—essentially a daiquiri with muddled spearmint. Any one of the hundreds of brands of rum will make for a different tasting cocktail. The amount of sugar and the particular type of sugar you use will drastically alter the flavor as well. The darker the rum, the richer and more flavorful your cocktail will be. My favorite mojito recipe makes a tart, minty cocktail with refreshing, honey-floral notes. If you can't find Charbay cane rum, 10 Cane is an excellent substitute.

1 1/2 ounces Charbay cane rum
3/4 ounce freshly squeezed lime juice
1/2 ounce Mint Simple Syrup (page 84)
3/4 ounce seltzer
10 spearmint leaves, cut into chiffonade

COMBINE the rum, juice, simple syrup, and seltzer in a mixing glass and stir. Add the spearmint and enough ice to fill the mixing glass, cover, and shake a few times. Pour into a tall collins glass to serve.

FRESH HERBS

Muddling is an effective way to release the flavors of large-leaf fresh herbs into a cocktail, but it tears up the herbs in a not-so-pretty fashion. Instead, I like to stack the leaves on top of one another and cut them into a chiffonade (thin slices) with a very sharp knife. This technique releases the flavor of the herbs as muddling does, and it also creates long, beautiful strands of herb that look fantastic clinging to the ice in your cocktail. Use this method with large-leaf basil, shiso, spearmint, anise hyssop, and large flower petals, like those of black-eyed Susans. For herbs with smaller leaves, like lemon verbena, cilantro, tarragon, small-leaf basils, and peppermint, simply give them a few firm taps with a muddler in the base of the mixing glass. If you muddle the herbs into a paste, it can ruin the flavor of your cocktail, so don't overdo it.

From left to right: Blackberry Lick and
Fraser River Sour (page 92).

BLACKBERRY LICK

MAKES 1 COCKTAIL

In early summer, Joel, Renee, and Sarah Kiff of Ridgeview Farms offer fresh olallieberries at the Healdsburg Farmers' Market. The berries are deep purple in color, perfectly tart, and full of rich berry flavor. Olallieberry season is short, sometimes lasting for less than one month, but cousins of the olallieberry, including marionberries, become available soon after from Sebastopol Berry Farm. Also around this time, wild blackberries start ripening on the outskirts of Healdsburg. I pick them daily, free of charge.

The Blackberry Lick stays on the Cyrus menu for as long as I can get these berries. The chiffonade of anise hyssop complements the blackberry, and simple syrup infused with essence of hyssop gives this complex cocktail a subtle menthol quality. If you don't want to go to the trouble of making the hyssop syrup, use plain simple syrup instead. The berry syrup also makes a nice addition to Westside Bellinis (page 95), mimosas, or a Kir royale.

3/4 ounce Hangar One Fraser River raspberry vodka

3/4 ounce vodka

1/2 ounce Purple Berry Syrup (see recipe)

1/2 ounce Hyssop Simple Syrup (see recipe) or simple syrup (see page 20)

3/4 ounce freshly squeezed lemon juice

3/4 ounce seltzer

5 anise hyssop leaves, cut into chiffonade

Anise hyssop leaves or blossoms, for garnish

Purple berries, for garnish (optional)

COMBINE the vodkas, syrups, and seltzer in a mixing glass and stir well. Add the chiffonade of anise hyssop and enough ice to fill the mixing glass. Cover and shake a few times. Pour into a tall collins glass and garnish with anise hyssop leaves and purple berries to serve.

continued

Purple Berry Syrup

MAKES ABOUT $^1/_2$ CUP (ENOUGH FOR ABOUT 8 COCKTAILS)

1 pound olallieberries, marionberries, or blackberries

Push the berries through a fine-mesh strainer or chinois into an airtight container; this takes a bit of effort. Be sure to scrape the outside of the strainer to get all of the strained berry matter into the container. The syrup will keep for 3 to 4 days refrigerated in an airtight container, and any leftovers make a delicious topper for toast or pancakes.

Hyssop Simple Syrup

MAKES $1^1/_2$ CUPS (ENOUGH FOR ABOUT 24 COCKTAILS)

$1^1/_2$ cups simple syrup, chilled (see page 20)
1 drop essential oil of hyssop

Combine the simple syrup and essential oil in an airtight container and shake well. The syrup will keep for 3 to 4 weeks refrigerated in the airtight container.

WHAT IS VERJUICE?

Verjuice (also *verjus*; literally, "green juice") is juice made from unripe wine grapes, generally picked at about 14 percent sugar by volume. There are many brands of red and white verjuice from both Napa and Sonoma counties. My two favorites are Terra Sonoma and Fusion from Napa Valley. In cooking, verjuice can be substituted wherever citrus juice or vinegar is called for, particularly when deglazing pans and making salad dressing. I like to use verjuice in cocktails with other acid components.

HUCK YU

MAKES 1 COCKTAIL

Wild huckleberries grow prodigiously in the forests on the Sonoma coast in late summer, so I take full advantage for this cocktail. The name comes from a combination of *huckleberries* and *yuzu*, a sour Japanese citrus juice available by the bottle. Vodka, white verjuice, limoncello, and sparkling wine round off this tart and complex berry cocktail. You can either make your own limoncello or buy a good-quality bottle from Italy.

1 ounce vodka

1/2 ounce limoncello (see page 12)

1 ounce white verjuice (see page 90)

1/4 ounce yuzu juice

1/4 ounce Huckleberry Syrup (see recipe)

2 ounces Prosecco or Cava

COMBINE the vodka, limoncello, juices, and syrup in a mixing glass and stir well. Add enough ice to fill the mixing glass, cover, and shake well. Strain into a champagne flute and add the sparkling wine very slowly to serve.

Huckleberry Syrup

MAKES ABOUT 1 CUP (ENOUGH FOR ABOUT 32 COCKTAILS)

1/2 pound fresh or frozen huckleberries

1/4 cup sugar

1/2 cup white verjuice (see page 90)

Combine the huckleberries, sugar, and verjuice in a stainless steel saucepan over high heat. Bring the mixture to a boil, stirring frequently, then reduce the heat to low and simmer for 10 minutes, until the berry skins have burst and the liquid is slightly reduced. Remove from the heat and press through a fine-mesh strainer or chinois into an airtight container. Allow the syrup to cool to at least room temperature before using. The syrup will keep for up to 2 weeks refrigerated in the airtight container; any leftovers are delicious on toast or pancakes.

FRASER RIVER SOUR

MAKES 1 COCKTAIL (see photo on page 88)

After combing the West Coast for the best-quality raspberries, Lance Winters of St. George Spirits decided that Meeker raspberries from Fraser River Valley in Washington State are superior to all others. Lance distills these special fruits to make raspberry vodka, eau de vie, and liqueur. Some of the berries are reserved for maceration and a very small amount is converted into juice to add flavor and color to the vodka and liqueur. The results are always extraordinary.

Since Lance's vodka is quite flavorful, I cut it with cane rum, which gives this drink a fuller body. The combination of fresh raspberries, tart lemon juice, lemon verbena, and an egg white creates a wonderful mouthfeel. If you rub the scented geranium leaf between your fingers before you drink, you get a wonderful aroma with your first sip.

5 lemon verbena leaves

1 egg white

³/₄ ounce Hangar One Fraser River raspberry vodka

³/₄ ounce 10 Cane or Charbay cane rum

³/₄ ounce freshly squeezed lemon juice

¹/₂ ounce Raspberry–Lemon Verbena Syrup (see recipe)

2 dashes Angostura bitters

Scented geranium leaf, for garnish

Purple basil blossoms or other edible flowers, for garnish

PLACE a V-shaped glass in the freezer to chill.

Place the lemon verbena leaves in the bottom of a mixing glass and tap a few times with a muddler. Add the egg white to the mixing glass, seal it up tight with a firm tap, and shake vigorously for 10 seconds, until white and frothy. Crack open the shaker and pour the mixture back into the mixing glass. Add the vodka, rum, juice, syrup, bitters, and enough ice to fill the mixing glass. Cover and shake vigorously for another 10 seconds. Strain into the chilled glass. After about 20 seconds, a nice head will form on top of the drink. Garnish with a geranium leaf and basil blossoms to serve.

Raspberry–Lemon Verbena Syrup

....

MAKES ABOUT 1 CUP (ENOUGH FOR ABOUT 16 COCKTAILS)

    1 cup simple syrup (see page 20)
    2 large or 3 small lemon verbena leaves
    ¼ cup fresh raspberries

Combine the simple syrup and lemon verbena in a saucepan over high heat. Bring the mixture to a boil and add the raspberries. Bring the mixture back to a boil, then reduce the heat to low and simmer for 5 minutes, or until the raspberries have fallen apart. Remove the syrup from the heat and let it rest for 15 minutes. Press through a fine-mesh strainer or chinois into an airtight container and allow the syrup to cool to at least room temperature before using. The syrup will keep for 1 week refrigerated in the airtight container.

From left to right: Westside Bellini and
Bella Ruffina (page 125).

WESTSIDE BELLINI

MAKES 1 COCKTAIL

A true Bellini must be made with white peaches. According to the Sullivans of Dry Creek Peach and Produce, the best options are the Snow King, Yukon King, and Arctic Gem varieties. When selecting white peaches, look for ripe, unbruised fruit with a rich red color around the pit; these will give your drink a beautiful pinkish hue. Although yellow peaches don't make good Bellinis, they do make attractive dehydrated peach chips that you can float atop your cocktail for garnish.

My Bellinis are made from fresh peach puree. After you puree and strain the peaches, the puree will be a gorgeous shade of pink for about twenty minutes, then it will slowly turn orange-brown due to oxidation. This doesn't affect the flavor of the drink, so don't be dismayed. If you want to preserve the color, especially if you're going to freeze any leftover puree, add $3/4$ teaspoon of powdered vitamin C to each cup of puree. My favorite garnishes for this cocktail are a dehydrated peach chip and bright little orange threads plucked from a fully bloomed safflower. However, the peach chip will do just fine on its own.

4 $1/2$ ounces chilled Prosecco
1 $1/2$ ounces White Peach Puree (see recipe)
1 Dehydrated Peach Chip, for garnish (see recipe)
Safflower threads, for garnish (optional)

PLACE a mixing glass and a V-shaped glass or champagne flute in the freezer to chill.

Combine the Prosecco and puree in the chilled mixing glass and stir vigorously. The mixture may fizz up quite a bit but should settle within a minute. Carefully pour into the chilled glass and garnish with a peach chip and safflower threads to serve.

continued

Variation: To make a pitcher of Bellinis, combine a 750 ml bottle of Prosecco with 7 ounces of peach puree. If you measure out a pitcher's worth of puree and freeze it in a freezer bag, you can have quick and easy Bellinis by breaking the frozen puree into small pieces and stirring it into the Prosecco. The frozen pieces will melt fairly quickly.

White Peach Puree

MAKES ABOUT 3 CUPS (ENOUGH FOR ABOUT 15 COCKTAILS)

About 5 ripe white peaches, pitted

1 ounce freshly squeezed lemon juice

$^1/_2$ ounce simple syrup (see page 20)

5 dashes Fee Brothers peach bitters (optional)

1 tablespoon powdered vitamin C (optional)

To make the puree, combine the peaches, juice, simple syrup, and bitters in a food processor and puree on medium speed until smooth. If necessary, puree the peaches in batches. Press the peach puree through a fine-mesh strainer or chinois into an airtight container. Stir in the vitamin C. Stored in the airtight container, the puree will keep for about 5 days in the refrigerator or about 2 months in the freezer. To use the frozen puree, set the sealed container in large bowl of warm water for 30 minutes, or until thawed.

Dehydrated Peach Chips

MAKES 3 TO 6 CHIPS

1 underripe or firm white or yellow peach

1 teaspoon Chinese Five-Spice Syrup (page 18) or simple syrup (see page 20)

3 to 6 small spearmint leaves

Using a sharp knife, cut as many $^1/_4$-inch-thick slices from either side of the peach pit as you can (sometimes you get 3 per side; sometimes you get 6.) If the slice is bruised at all (and peaches do bruise very easily), it's not suitable for dehydrating.

If using a food dehydrator, spray the trays with vegetable oil or lightly oil them with a paper towel. Lay the peach slices on the rack. Put one drop of honey or syrup on each piece and gently press a spearmint leaf into it until it adheres to the peach slice. Dehydrating will take 24 to 36 hours, depending on the thickness of the slice.

If using the oven, preheat it to 150°F. Lay the peach slices on a silicone mat and follow the instructions above to construct the garnish. Place the silicone mat on the center rack in the oven and bake for 5 hours, until almost all of the moisture is gone. Set the chips on a wire rack to cool. They will be warm, soft, and limp for a few minutes and will harden as they cool, just like cookies fresh from the oven. Stored in an airtight container, the peach chips will keep for about 3 days.

PLUM DANDY

MAKES 1 COCKTAIL

Proportions are particularly critical with the Plum Dandy; it's important that every ingredient announce itself, and there are many voices to be heard here. Japanese plum wines aren't actually made from plums, but rather from a plumlike fruit called an *ume*. My preferred plum wine is Choya Ume Blanc, but there are plenty of suitable plum wines available at Japanese markets. Jasmine blossoms are very delicate. Shaking them in the cocktail would destroy them, which is why I add them at the end. Keep the jasmine blossoms in a bowl of cold water until you use them; they'll last for twelve to twenty-four hours, after which the white pigment dissolves, leaving you with clear flowers that will disappear in the cocktail.

5 to 8 peppermint leaves

$1/2$ ounce Hangar One mandarin orange blossom vodka

$1/2$ ounce vodka

$3/4$ ounce Choya Ume Blanc

$1/2$ ounce Chinese Five-Spice Syrup (page 18)

$3/4$ ounce freshly squeezed lemon juice

$3/4$ ounce seltzer

8 to 10 small red plums, or Bing or Rainier cherries, pitted and halved

10 to 15 jasmine blossoms

PLACE the peppermint leaves in the bottom of a mixing glass and tap a few times with a muddler. Add the vodkas, Ume Blanc, syrup, juice, and seltzer, and stir well. Add the cherry pieces and enough ice to fill the mixing glass, cover, and shake a few times. Pour into a tall collins glass. Set the jasmine blossoms on top of the drink and, using a straw or a knife, carefully push them down into the glass so the blossoms, peppermint leaves, and cherry pieces are evenly distributed throughout the drink.

TOMATO WATER AND TOMATO JUICE

Both tomato water and tomato juice begin as pureed peak-of-season tomatoes. They are so delicious (especially when made from heirloom tomatoes) and remarkably easy to make that you may never buy canned tomato juice again. There are hundreds of varieties of heirloom tomatoes in an amazing array of colors, sizes, and shapes. When you make heirloom tomato juice cocktails, play with these variances to give your drinks some style. For instance, I like the color of my base tomato juice to be different from that of the pieces of tomato floating in the drink.

Tomato water is simply tomato puree that has been placed in a cloth-lined strainer or chinois and suspended over a container to strain. After 24 hours, the water in the tomatoes will filter through the cloth and into the container. The tomato water will be mostly clear with a slight hue of color coming from whichever variety of tomato you've chosen. Both tomato water and tomato puree need a healthy dose of salt to bring out their flavors.

Heirloom Tomato Juice

MAKES ABOUT 5 CUPS (ENOUGH FOR ABOUT 20 COCKTAILS)

$2^1/_2$ pounds ripe heirloom tomatoes, at room temperature

$^1/_2$ to 1 teaspoon kosher salt

Core the tomatoes and place them in a blender with the salt. Puree the tomatoes until smooth, then strain through a fine-mesh strainer or chinois, pressing the puree through the screen with a ladle or large spoon. The tomato juice will keep for up to 3 days if refrigerated in an airtight container.

Heirloom Tomato Water

MAKES 2 TO 4 CUPS (ENOUGH FOR 10 TO 20 COCKTAILS)

2 1/2 pounds ripe heirloom tomatoes, at room temperature

1/2 to 1 teaspoon kosher salt

Core the tomatoes and place them in a blender with the salt. Puree the tomatoes until smooth. Line a fine-mesh strainer or chinois with at least ten layers of fine-mesh cheese-cloth and set the strainer over an uncovered airtight container in the refrigerator. Pour the tomato puree into the strainer and allow it to drain through the cheesecloth. It will take about 12 hours to fully drain, but you'll start to see some movement after the first hour. It should drain at the rate of about 1 drop per second and should be almost clear. The tomato water will keep for up to 3 days if refrigerated in the airtight container.

From left to right: The Upstairs Neighbor (page 105) and Celery Mary.

CELERY MARY

MAKES 1 COCKTAIL

My variation on a Bloody Mary uses young celery leaves and juice made from fresh heirloom tomatoes. Pickled celery root looks and tastes great in this drink, but if there were ever a drink to load up with pickled goods, this is the one, so be creative. For the all-important savory component, I use Apple Farm apple balsamic vinegar from the town of Philo in Northern California's Mendocino County. This versatile vinegar isn't a true balsamic vinegar, being made with apples rather than Trebbiano grapes. Still, it tastes as good in a seasonal cocktail as it does on a roasted pork loin. Handmade by the original owners of Napa Valley's French Laundry restaurant, it combines the flavors of caramel, vinegar, apple, and spice. If you can't find this vinegar, use any well-aged Italian balsamic vinegar instead. Whatever you do, please don't use A1 Steak Sauce or Worcestershire sauce.

1 1/2 ounces vodka

2 ounces Heirloom Tomato Juice
   (see page 100)

1/2 ounce freshly squeezed lemon juice

1/2 ounce Apple Farm apple balsamic vinegar

Pinch of celery salt

Pinch of kosher salt

1/4 teaspoon freshly ground black pepper

15 Pickled Celery Root Threads (see recipe)

13 young celery leaves

COMBINE the vodka, juices, vinegar, celery salt, salt, and pepper in a mixing glass and stir well. Add the celery root pieces, 10 of the celery leaves, and enough ice to fill the mixing glass. Cover and shake a few times. Pour into a tall collins glass and garnish with the remaining 3 celery leaves to serve.

continued

Pickled Celery Root Threads

MAKES ABOUT 150 PIECES (ENOUGH FOR ABOUT 10 COCKTAILS)

1 quart Ultimate Pickling Liquid (page 52)
1 pound celery root

In a stainless steel saucepan over high heat, bring the pickling liquid to a boil. Trim the outside edges of the celery root to produce an unblemished cube. Slice the cube into $1/8$-inch-thick pieces, then slice the squares into matchstick-size pieces. Place the celery pieces in an airtight container and add the boiling pickling liquid. Cool in the refrigerator before using. The celery root will keep for up to 2 months refrigerated in the airtight container. If you have leftovers, the crunchy celery root is great in salads as well.

THE UPSTAIRS NEIGHBOR

MAKES 1 COCKTAIL (see photo on page 102)

Imagine a *Caprese* salad (without the mozzarella!) and you have the Upstairs Neighbor. It's light, refreshing, and full of the fresh flavors of summer. Use an extensively aged balsamic vinegar to add a complex and savory quality to the drink. Multicolored cherry tomatoes and green and purple basil make this one of my most eye-catching concoctions. If you can't find small-leaf basil, cut large-leaf basil into a chiffonade before muddling.

1/2 lemon, for rim

2 tablespoons red sea salt, for rim

10 small purple opal basil leaves

10 small sweet Italian basil leaves

1 1/2 ounces vodka

1 1/2 ounces Heirloom Tomato Water
   (see page 101)

1/4 ounce freshly squeezed lemon juice

3/4 teaspoon balsamic vinegar

5 small cherry tomatoes, halved

1/4 teaspoon kosher salt

1/4 teaspoon freshly ground black pepper

RUB the lemon half around the rim of a tall collins glass and shake off any excess juice. Dip the glass into the red sea salt to coat the rim (see page 38).

Place the basil leaves in the bottom of a mixing glass and tap a few times with a muddler. Add the vodka, tomato water, juice, balsamic vinegar, tomatoes, salt, and pepper, and stir well. Add enough ice to fill the mixing glass, cover, and shake a few times. Pour into the salt-rimmed glass to serve.

CREOLE WATERMELON

MAKES 1 COCKTAIL

I like to think of this drink as the more sophisticated way to experience vodka-soaked watermelon—a popular tradition at colleges and universities. The drink is reminiscent of a refreshing watermelon gazpacho prepared with a Creole touch. If you don't use a good-quality melon, this drink has the potential to be boring and watery, so be sure to look for fruits with deep, rich color, and sample before you buy, if at all possible. Try using small water-melons of different colors, choosing one color for the juice and another color for the frozen watermelon pieces.

1 (3 to 5-pound) ripe heirloom watermelon

15 cilantro leaves

3/4 ounce Hangar One Kaffir lime vodka

3/4 ounce vodka

1/2 ounce freshly squeezed lime juice

1 1/2 ounces Watermelon Juice (see recipe)

1/4 ounce simple syrup (see page 20)

1/4 teaspoon chili powder, plus more for garnish

1/8 teaspoon kosher salt, plus more for garnish

1/4 teaspoon freshly ground black pepper, plus more for garnish

CUT the watermelon crosswise into 1/3-inch-thick round slices, then cut each slice into 8 wedges. Line a baking sheet small enough to fit into the freezer with a layer of parchment paper. Lay the watermelon wedges on the parchment paper about 1/2 inch apart. If you run out of room on the first layer, lay another sheet of parchment paper on top of the first and continue to lay down the watermelon wedges. Cover the wedges with plastic wrap and place the baking sheet in the freezer for at least 2 hours, until the wedges are frozen.

Place a V-shaped glass in the freezer to chill.

Put 10 of the cilantro leaves in the bottom of a mixing glass and tap a few times with a muddler. Add the vodkas, juices, simple syrup, chili powder, salt, and pepper, and stir well. Add enough ice to fill the mixing glass, cover, and shake hard for 7 seconds. Strain into the chilled glass and add 5 or 6 frozen watermelon wedges and the remaining 5 cilantro leaves. Dust the top of the cocktail with a little chili powder, salt, and pepper to serve.

continued

Watermelon Juice

....

MAKES 2 TO 3 CUPS (ENOUGH FOR 10 TO 15 COCKTAILS)

1 or 2 (3 to 5-pound) ripe heirloom watermelons

Cut the watermelon crosswise into $^{1}/_{3}$-inch-thick round slices. Remove the rind and cut the watermelon into cubes. Press the cubes through a fine-mesh strainer or chinois to remove the fibrous material. If you have leftover watermelon juice, drink it straight over ice with a little salt. Watermelon juice is the most perishable liquid I've worked with. Even if you refrigerate it, it will last less than 24 hours.

PIMM'S CUP

MAKES 1 COCKTAIL

It's a shame that this classic British cocktail doesn't appear on more menus, because its savory, herbaceous, and citrus flavors are delicious. I prefer to use Sonoma Sparkler sparkling lemonade because it's delicious and made in Healdsburg, but you can use any all-natural sparkling lemonade instead. The traditional Pimm's cup calls for a cucumber garnish, but because I like cucumbers a lot, I go a little crazy with them here. You'll have quite a few cucumbers left over for a salad or cucumber sandwiches.

1 English cucumber

1 Armenian cucumber

1 small lemon cucumber

$1\frac{1}{2}$ ounces Pimm's No. 1

3 ounces Sonoma Sparkler sparkling lemonade

1 ounce seltzer

1 (16-inch-long) orange zest

USING a potato peeler or sharp paring knife, carefully peel the English cucumber in long strands and reserve the peels. Slice the Armenian cucumber into $1/4$-inch medallions. Cut the lemon cucumber into 8 pieces. Put 4 of the lemon cucumber pieces and a few ice cubes into a mixing glass and muddle them down to a pulp. Add the Pimm's, lemonade, and seltzer and stir well. Add enough ice to fill the mixing glass, cover, and shake a few times.

Strain the liquid into another mixing glass and add 5 of the reserved English cucumber peels, the orange zest, and 10 of the Armenian cucumber pieces and stir well. Add enough ice to fill the mixing glass, cover, and shake well. Pour into a tall collins glass to serve.

CHAPTER 4

FALL

AUTUMN is harvest time and the peak season for great produce. Many of the herbs, flowers, and vegetables from the spring and summer seasons are still available, but new things that I've waited all year for are finally ripe for the picking, including apples, pears, wine grapes, pomegranates, and peppers.

Northern California's Sonoma, Lake, and Mendocino counties have been famous for their apples and pears for more than a hundred years. These delicious fruits start appearing in August, when the first white wine grapes are picked. The recent popularity of sour apple martinis has unfortunately made us forget that *real* apple products make delicious fall drinks. Apple juice blends well with vodka, gin, rum, and brandy, and thin slices of apple and pear can be dehydrated or baked into attractive and edible garnishes (see page 113). My favorite variety of apple to dehydrate, the Pink Pearl, has a lovely blush hue, but there are dozens of heirloom apples I work with throughout the fall.

Wine grapes don't have to be used just for wine making; many wineries bottle unfermented (nonalcoholic) juices and unripe juice (verjuice; see page 90), both of which I use in cocktails as well as cooking. Making your own fresh wine-grape juice from scratch (see page 128) is a fairly simple process, but it can be a messy one if you're working with red wine grapes. I make my own

red wine juice for the Grapes of Roth (page 27), one of the most popular and beautiful drinks we serve.

Several different growers provide Cyrus with local pomegranates, including Lou Preston, a local winemaker and organic-sustainable guru; Paul and Yael Bernier, two of the original founders of the Healdsburg Farmers' Market; and Andre Pinel and Andrea Burke, two of the restaurant's captains. As with citrus juice, freshly squeezed pomegranates yield an extraordinary juice full of color and flavor. It is remarkably better in quality than any pasteurized juice from a bottle.

Peppers, like tomatoes, add a delicious savory element to cocktails. Available in quintessential autumn colors such as red, orange, and yellow, peppers add a little sweetness and sometimes a nice spicy bite, like in the Irian Jaya (page 131).

With the grape harvest in full swing during the fall season, activity in the bar and around the Healdsburg town square kicks up a few notches. The abundance of ripe produce keeps me on my toes as I strive to come up with new uses for the beautiful ingredients growing all around me. As the fall season winds down and the shorter, cooler days of winter appear, once again I make changes to the Cyrus bar menu. Fresh borage flowers and succulent tomatoes are replaced with boxes of bright yellow, green, and orange citrus fruits—and thus begins another delicious season of cocktails.

DEHYDRATING FRUIT

Dehydrated slices of fruit make excellent cocktail garnishes. Whether you use a food dehydrator or the oven, starchy fruits such as apples, pears, figs, and persimmons work best. I've also had great success with stone fruit, including many varieties of peaches, plums, and apricots. Dehydrated citrus looks attractive but is almost always too acidic unless blanched first. Even then, citrus generally becomes too hard to eat.

If you're using a food dehydrator, spray the dehydrating racks with vegetable oil or rub them lightly with a paper towel dipped in vegetable oil. Tap out any excess oil. Cut the fruit into $1/8$- to $1/4$-inch-thick slices, then dip them in simple syrup (see page 20). The simple syrup adds a little necessary sweetness and prevents the fruit from browning. Shake off any excess syrup and lay the slices on the racks. Dehydrating usually takes 24 to 48 hours, depending on the fruit and how thin you've sliced it.

If you don't have a food dehydrator, you can bake thin slices of fruit in your oven at a very low temperature for a similar result. The tricky part is to keep the fruit from turning brown or burning. If you're using the oven, line a baking sheet with a silicone mat. Follow the instructions above to slice the fruit, dip the slices in simple syrup, and lay them on the mat. Place the baking sheet on the center rack in the oven and bake the slices at 150°F for 5 hours, or until they have the consistency of a thin, warm cookie (hard around the edges and soft in the middle). Watch the slices carefully; if they start to turn brown, take them out of the oven or turn down the heat. Remove the baking sheet from the oven and allow the slices to cool. The fruit will harden quickly but still retain some moisture.

AUTUMN APPLE

MAKES 1 COCKTAIL

Many people who have had the Autumn Apple say that it actually tastes like fall. The classic combination of spicy ginger and tart baked apple flavors pairs remarkably well with our local Germain-Robin apple brandy. This brandy is made like a well-aged Cognac except the distiller begins with apple cider instead of grape wine. To complement the tart cocktail, a thin layer of apple foam is added after the drink has been strained into the glass. This foam becomes a cloud on which to float a dehydrated apple chip, a baked and browned apple chip, a sprinkle of cinnamon-sugar, and a few marigold petals.

Apple foam, for garnish

1 1/2 ounces Germain-Robin apple brandy

1/4 ounce freshly squeezed lemon juice

1/2 ounce Nana Mae's Gravenstein apple juice

1/2 ounce Sonoma Sparkler sparkling apple cider

1/4 ounce Ginger Simple Syrup (see recipe)

2 Dehydrated Apple Chips, for garnish (see recipe)

Cinnamon, for garnish (optional)

Sugar, for garnish (optional)

Marigold petals, for garnish

PLACE a V-shaped glass in the freezer to chill. Follow the instructions on page 29 to prepare and chill the apple foam using apple juice as the base.

Combine the apple brandy, juices, cider, and syrup in a mixing glass and stir well. Add enough ice to fill the mixing glass, cover, and shake hard for 7 seconds. Strain into the chilled glass, and apply a thin layer of apple foam to the top. Place the apple chips on top of the foam and sprinkle a little cinnamon and sugar on top. Carefully set 3 or 4 marigold petals on the foam to serve.

continued

Ginger Simple Syrup

· ·

MAKES ³/₄ CUP (ENOUGH FOR ABOUT 24 COCKTAILS)

> ³/₄ cup simple syrup, chilled (see page 20)
> 1 drop essential oil of ginger

Combine the simple syrup and essential oil in an airtight container and shake well. The syrup will keep for 3 to 4 weeks refrigerated in the airtight container.

Dehydrated Apple Chips

· ·

MAKES ABOUT 8 CHIPS (ENOUGH FOR 4 COCKTAILS)

> 1 small apple
> ¹/₂ cup simple syrup (see page 20)
> Cinnamon, for sprinkling
> Sugar, for sprinkling

Using a sharp knife or mandolin, cut as many ¹/₄-inch-thick slices from the apple as you can, removing the seeds.

If using a food dehydrator, spray the trays with vegetable oil or lightly oil them with a paper towel. Dip the apple slices in the simple syrup (to prevent browning) and shake off any excess syrup. Lay the slices on the rack. Sprinkle each slice with a little bit of cinnamon and sugar. Dehydrating will take 24 to 36 hours, depending on the thickness of the slice (see page 113).

If using the oven, preheat it to 150°F. Lay the apple slices on a silicone mat and sprinkle each with a little bit of cinnamon and sugar. Place the silicone mat on the center rack in the oven and bake for 5 hours, until almost all of the moisture is gone. Set the chips on a wire rack to cool. They will be warm, soft, and limp for a few minutes and will harden as they cool, just like cookies fresh from the oven. Stored in an airtight container, the chips will keep for 2 to 3 days.

HOT BUTTERED RUM

MAKES 1 COCKTAIL

This classic drink appears on the Cyrus cocktail menu after the first truly cold night of autumn. Rich and delicious, it will warm you to the bone. This recipe makes a richer hot buttered rum than you may have had in the past, further enhanced with lots of holiday spice flavors layered through the buttery cream. My choice of rum is Charbay Tahitian vanilla rum, but any good-quality dark or aged rum would be a nice substitute. This drink is also great without the rum.

3 ounces Hot Buttered Rum Batter (see recipe)

3 ounces boiling water

$1^1/_2$ ounces Charbay Tahitian vanilla rum

Whole nutmeg, for garnish

COMBINE the batter with boiling water as described below, then add the rum and stir to mix. Using a microplane grater, shave a little nutmeg on top. Always serve this drink with a spoon, as the butter may separate from the batter a bit and need to be stirred back in.

Hot Buttered Rum Batter

MAKES ABOUT $5^1/_2$ CUPS (ENOUGH FOR 15 COCKTAILS)

3 whole nutmeg pods

3 tablespoons allspice berries

3 (3-inch) cinnamon sticks, broken into pieces

1 cup whipping cream

$1^1/_2$ pints vanilla bean ice cream

$1/_2$ cup granulated sugar

$1/_2$ cup firmly packed brown sugar

$1/_2$ teaspoon kosher salt

1 pound (4 sticks) unsalted butter

Place the nutmeg pods in a towel and break them into pieces with a hammer or other blunt object. Place the nutmeg pieces, allspice, and cinnamon in a spice or coffee grinder and process to a coarse powder. Heat a stainless steel pan over medium heat and follow the instructions on

continued

page 20 to toast the spices. Once the spices are aromatic, add the cream and ice cream. Bring the mixture to a boil and stir in the sugars and the salt. Cut the butter into 10 cubes and stir them in a few at a time until melted completely. Remove the mixture from the heat. If you're going to use all of the batter right away, mix in an equal amount of boiling water. The batter is now ready to use.

If you want to freeze some of the batter for later use, don't add the boiling water. Place the batter in a bowl set over a larger bowl of ice and stir occasionally until the batter reaches room temperature. Pour the batter into silicone ice cube trays or measure out 3-ounce quantities and store in individual freezer bags. To serve, place 3 batter cubes or 3 ounces of batter with an equal amount of water in a saucepan over medium-high heat. When the mixture boils, pour it into a coffee mug, add the rum, and stir. Shave a little nutmeg on top and drink up!

MARASCHINO LIQUEUR AND AMARENA CHERRIES

A common bar ingredient for well over a hundred years, maraschino liqueur was originally produced from the juice, pits, and leaves of the wild marasca cherry. Native to Dalmatia but usually produced in Italy, this aromatic liqueur made its way to the United States and was used in cocktails until the start of Prohibition, after which it became illegal.

Both before and after Prohibition, producers brined and bleached domestic Queen Anne and Rainer cherries with a sulfur dioxide solution, preserved them in sugar syrup, stained them with artificial food coloring, and flavored them with artificial almond flavoring. The result: the bright red maraschino cherries we all begged for in our Shirley Temples. By the time Prohibition ended, these imitation maraschino cherries had become so popular that real maraschino liqueur never really made a comeback—something I'm trying to change.

While contemporary maraschino cherries might have sentimental value, they don't taste nearly as good as another cherry product, an Italian variety called *amarena*. These wild cherries are processed according to a secret recipe that goes back generations and then preserved in a semi-candied syrup without alcohol. They are richly flavored, beautifully textured, and entirely natural. My favorite brands are Toschi and Fabbri; they are expensive and difficult to find, but the search is worth it if you're up for the challenge. Try an Italian specialty foods store, or do an online search by brand.

POMIRANIAN

MAKES 1 COCKTAIL

This drink is made with pomegranate juice enhanced with Iranian spices. Although you could use dried and toasted spices to prepare the pomegranate juice, in this case I think essential oils work just as well and require less effort. The PomIranian is a tart cocktail with many layers of spice—perfect for autumn.

10 to 15 peppermint leaves

3/4 ounce Hangar One mandarin orange blossom vodka

3/4 ounce vodka

1/2 ounce freshly squeezed lime juice

3/4 ounce Spiced Pomegranate Juice (see recipe)

1/4 ounce simple syrup (see page 20)

Black-eyed Susan petals, cut into chiffonade

Peppermint sprig, for garnish

Amaranth spear, for garnish

PLACE the peppermint in the bottom of a mixing glass and tap a few times with a muddler. Add the vodkas, juices, and simple syrup, and stir well. Add a small pinch of black-eyed Susan threads and enough ice to fill the mixing glass, cover, and shake a few times. Pour into a tall collins glass and garnish with the peppermint sprig, amaranth spear, and a few more threads of black-eyed Susan.

continued

| 123 |

Spiced Pomegranate Juice

....

MAKES 1$\frac{1}{3}$ CUPS (ENOUGH FOR ABOUT 14 COCKTAILS)

> 4 large, ripe pomegranates or 1$\frac{1}{3}$ cups 100 percent pomegranate juice
>
> 1 drop essential oil of cardamom
>
> 1 drop essential oil of nutmeg
>
> 1 drop essential oil of black pepper

Juice the pomegranates using a manual or electric juicer (see page 10). Strain the juice through a fine-mesh strainer or chinois to remove any solids. Place the juice and the essential oils in an airtight container and shake well to combine. The juice will keep for up to 1 week refrigerated in the airtight container.

BELLA RUFFINA

MAKES 1 COCKTAIL (see photo on page 94)

The deep crimson color of this cocktail makes it a festive number for holiday parties. Braquetto d'Aqui is a low-alcohol sparkling red wine from Italy with its very own *Denominazione di Origine Controllata e Garantita* (DOCG), which means it has been produced in a traditional and consistent way in a designated geographical area within Italy. And that means it's like nothing else in the world. Carpano Antica is a full-flavored sweet vermouth that complements the herbaceous qualities in the sparkling wine; you could also use Punt e Mes, Cocchi Barolo Chinato, or another high-quality sweet Italian vermouth. The orange bitters give the drink a lingering finish and complex aromatics.

4 ounces Braquetto d'Aqui
1 ounce Carpano Antica vermouth
1 dash orange bitters
1 Amarena cherry, for garnish

COMBINE the sparkling wine, vermouth, and bitters in a champagne flute and stir gently. Drop the cherry into the bottom of the glass to serve.

GRAPES OF ROTH

MAKES 1 COCKTAIL

During the harvest months, I'm fortunate to get some extra wine grapes from friends like Ted and Nicole Simpkins of Lancaster Vineyards and the Newman family, both in Alexander Valley. At Cyrus, we make our own juice from Cabernet or Merlot grapes, and also freeze some of the small bunches of grapes to use as a garnish in this cocktail. A local, unripe red grape juice (red verjuice) is combined with aromatic, high-acid yuzu juice (from a Japanese citrus fruit; available by the bottle from Asian groceries) to form a complex, tangy drink tempered by a thin layer of silky, rich grape foam. I set the frozen, edible grapes on the rim of the glass and garnish with tiny orange safflower threads. To make a true Grapes of Roth, you have to use our local Roth vodka, but you could also use another high-quality unflavored vodka in this cocktail.

Cabernet or Merlot grapes, for garnish

Cabernet foam, for garnish (see page 28)

1 tablespoon ground cardamom

2 tablespoons sugar

1 1/2 ounces Roth vodka

1/2 ounce red verjuice (see page 90)

1/4 ounce yuzu juice

1/4 ounce freshly squeezed lemon juice

1/2 ounce Cabernet Grape Juice (see recipe)

10 safflower threads, for garnish

PLACE the grapes and a V-shaped glass in the freezer to chill. Follow the instructions on page 28 to prepare and chill the Cabernet foam, using Cabernet juice as the base. Combine the cardamom and sugar in a small bowl and set aside.

Combine the vodka, verjuice, and juices in a mixing glass and stir well. Add enough ice to fill the mixing glass, cover, and shake hard for 7 seconds. Strain into the chilled glass and apply a thin layer of Cabernet foam on top. Hang the frozen grapes on the rim of the glass and lightly sprinkle with the cardamom–sugar mixture. Carefully position the safflower threads on the frozen grapes to serve.

continued

Cabernet Grape Juice

....

MAKES ABOUT 2 CUPS (ENOUGH FOR ABOUT 10 COCKTAILS)

    1 pound Cabernet grapes, rinsed

In a saucepan over high heat, combine the grapes (stems included) with a scant $\frac{1}{2}$ cup of water. When the water is just hot to the touch, start smashing down the grapes with a potato masher. Bring the water to a boil and cook until all of the grapes have burst and the liquid becomes dark purple, about 10 minutes. Reduce the heat if the grapes start to splatter. Remove the pot from the heat and pour the pulp into an airtight container. Cool in the refrigerator and let it rest for 24 hours to leach out even more color from the skins. Strain the juice through a fine-mesh strainer or chinois to remove the stems, skins, and other solids. Stored in the airtight container, the juice will keep for 1 week in the refrigerator or 2 months in the freezer. This same method can be used to make white grape juice. Gewürztraminer and Muscat are my favorite varietals.

EDIBLE FLOWERS

At Cyrus, we use dozens of varieties of edible flowers in our cocktails throughout the year. Some of the flowers blossom only once in spring, some blossom again in the fall, and others produce flowers continuously throughout the warm-weather months. The tiniest of blossoms, such as individual rosemary or basil flowers, are the perfect size to float atop silky foams. With midsize flowers, like dianthus and marigold, I use individual petals. With the biggest edible flowers, like black-eyed Susans, I roll up the petals and cut them into thin strips. I always try to match the right flower to the right drink, considering color, size, aroma, taste, and sensibility. One thing is certain: taking the time to carefully garnish cocktails with these little miracles of nature will produce outstanding results.

Following is a list of just some of the edible flowers I use in my cocktails: amaranth spears, anise hyssop blossoms, basil blossoms (purple or Thai), black-eyed Susan petals, blanketflower petals, borage flowers, cosmos, dianthus flowers, glowering maple, hollyhock, hummingbird mint blossoms, jasmine blossoms, lavender, certain marigold petals, rosemary blossoms, roses, safflower threads, sage blossoms, scented geranium leaves, snapdragons, sunflower petals, and zucchini blossoms.

IRIAN JAYA

MAKES 1 COCKTAIL

Irian Jaya is the name of a region of Indonesia, and the flavors of this cocktail—chile, ginger, Kaffir lime, and lemongrass—are common in Indonesian cuisine. Nardello peppers are long, thin, mild-flavored peppers with a deep red color. If you love spicy drinks, like I do, you can ratchet up the heat in the spicy pickled peppers by adding more chiles. When these spicy pickled peppers are added to the cocktail, some of the pickling liquid gets into the drink as well. This is a nice complement to the tart lime juice, the sweet lemongrass, and the aromatic Kaffir lime flavors from the fresh leaf and the Hangar One vodka.

3/4 ounce Hangar One Kaffir lime vodka

3/4 ounce vodka

3/4 ounce freshly squeezed lime juice

1/4 ounce simple syrup (see page 20)

3/4 ounce Bundaberg or Cock'n Bull ginger beer

1 1/2 tablespoons Pickled Nardello Peppers (see recipe)

15 pieces Candied Lemongrass (see recipe)

3 Kaffir lime leaves, cut into long chiffonade

COMBINE the vodkas, juice, syrup, and ginger beer in a mixing glass and stir well. Add the peppers, lemongrass, lime leaves, and enough ice to fill the mixing glass. Cover and shake a few times. Pour into a tall collins glass to serve.

continued

Pickled Nardello Peppers

....

MAKES 1 QUART (ENOUGH FOR ABOUT 16 COCKTAILS)

1 1/3 cups Ultimate Pickling Liquid (page 52)

1 pound Nardello peppers

1 Fresno chile or 2 small red serrano chiles

Heat the pickling liquid in a stainless steel saucepan over high heat until it boils. Meanwhile, slice the peppers into 1/8-inch-thick rings and shake out the seeds. Slice the chile into 1/8-inch-thick rings, and place them, seeds included, in an airtight container with the peppers. Pour the pickling liquid over the peppers and chiles and cool in the refrigerator before using. The pickled peppers will keep for 1 month refrigerated. These are also a great accompaniment to a charcuterie platter in place of cornichons.

Candied Lemongrass

....

MAKES ABOUT 150 PIECES (ENOUGH FOR 10 COCKTAILS)

1 cup simple syrup (see page 20)

1/2 pound lemongrass

Heat the syrup in a saucepan over high heat until it boils. Meanwhile, remove both ends of the lemongrass, leaving just the whitish purple part. Slice the stalk at a 45-degree angle into 1/8-inch disks. Add the lemongrass rings to the saucepan and bring the syrup back to a boil. Reduce the heat to low and simmer for 5 minutes, until the lemongrass has softened a bit. Remove the pan from heat and allow the lemongrass to cool slightly. Pour the lemongrass and syrup into an airtight container and cool in the refrigerator before using. The candied lemongrass will only keep for 72 hours if refrigerated (after that it gets cloudy and gooey). Although only the lemongrass is called for in this recipe, the syrup itself is wonderful for making Lemongrass Lemonade (page 133) or hot tea.

LEMONGRASS LEMONADE

MAKES 1 COCKTAIL

After making the candied lemongrass for your Irian Jaya (page 131) cocktail, you'll have some tasty lemongrass simple syrup left over. Rather than tossing it out, I like to make this minty, sweet lemonade with it.

2 ounces freshly squeezed lemon juice

2 ounces lemongrass simple syrup (see Candied Lemongrass, page 132)

4 ounces seltzer

10 spearmint leaves, cut into chiffonade

Lemongrass stalk, for garnish

COMBINE the juice, simple syrup, and seltzer in a mixing glass and stir well. Add the spearmint threads and enough ice to fill the mixing glass, cover, and shake a few times. Pour into a tall collins glass and garnish with the lemongrass stalk to serve.

PAINFUL PUNCH

MAKES ABOUT 3 GALLONS

This punch was originally inspired by a sangria recipe I learned from my friend David Hanna. More flavorful and higher in alcohol than your average sangria, this punch uses inexpensive wine from Spain. My two favorite brands are Protocolo and Borsao, both of which provide a juicy, full-flavored foundation for spiced juice and liquors. The punch has a tendency to be rather tannic tasting, so I add simple syrup cup by cup until the sweetness is just right.

One of the most tragic downfalls of a party punch is overdilution, which happens when the punch is chilled with fast-melting ice cubes. I serve this punch either prechilled with ice on the side, or with one large piece of block ice in the bowl and ice on the side.

3 whole nutmeg pods

3 tablespoons whole allspice berries

3 (3-inch) cinnamon sticks, broken into pieces

2 quarts orange juice

2 quarts pineapple juice

12 (750 ml) bottles Spanish red wine

1 (750 ml) bottle VSOP Cognac

1 (750 ml) bottle Myers dark rum

1 to 5 cups simple syrup (see page 20), to taste

10 oranges, sliced into wedges

PLACE the nutmeg pods in a cloth napkin and break them into pieces with a hammer or other blunt object. Combine the nutmeg, allspice, and cinnamon in a large stainless steel saucepan over medium heat. Follow the instructions on page 20 to toast the spices until aromatic, about 5 minutes. Add the juices and bring the mixture to a boil. Reduce the heat to low and simmer until the mixture is reduced by one-third, about 30 minutes. Remove the pot from the heat and strain the liquid through a fine-mesh strainer or chinois into a container large enough to hold all of the punch. Discard the spices.

Add the wine, Cognac, and rum, and stir well. Add the simple syrup 1 cup at a time until the tannins are tamed. Add the orange slices, cover the container, and place in the refrigerator to chill. To serve, transfer the mixture to a large glass punch bowl with a ladle. Serve the ice on the side.

MEET THE FARMERS

THE Healdsburg Farmers' Market, held in the plaza on Tuesdays and in the parking lot behind the Hotel Healdsburg on Saturdays, is a very special place. Most of the sellers are local: you can buy cheese from Pug's Leap Dairy out on Dry Creek Road, soap from Healdsburg Soap Company, locally raised meats from several producers, and fruits and vegetables from dozens of local growers. Some of these growers are full-time farmers, and others are retired folks who grow to supplement their income. Many have been coming to the market since it was founded as a co-op in 1979.

At that time, it was actually illegal to organize a market outside of the grocery store model, and it took many years and many determined people to make the market a reality. Tom Peterson, Paul Bernier, Granger Brown, Doug Stout, and a handful of others felt the town deserved the opportunity to produce and sell some of its own food. This food would be fresh, grown or raised by familiar faces, and carried to the market from a few miles away instead of trucked from far-off places using fossil-fueled vehicles. This concept is all the rage nowadays, but these folks were trying to do it during the age of disco.

Even after getting permission from the state to legally sell locally grown goods to their own community, the old-time vendors that I've spoken with agree that it wasn't until the early 1990s that the local community turned out in enough numbers to make the market consistently profitable. There is no doubt that Healdsburg loves its two weekly farmers' markets now. A walk through the crowded aisles is a ritual for many residents here; it's a chance to catch up with friends and talk about what tastes good this week and what will be ready next week. People all over the world have been going to market for thousands of years, and in the United States, we are slowly but surely beginning to reject the false convenience of the modern supermarket. The Healdsburg Farmers' Market proves that, in some regions, you could eat mostly organic, local food grown by people whose first names you know, for many of the months of the year. That is certainly food for thought.

Following is a short introduction to the people with whom I have worked who sell at the Healdsburg Farmers' Market. Many are not farmers by trade, but rather friends who sell, trade, or give me the beautiful ingredients I use at Cyrus throughout the year.

LA BONNE TERRE

Bert and Mary Villemaire (see photo below) live on Bailhache Avenue, about a quarter mile from my house. They've been retired for about ten years and grow produce for the Saturday farmers' market as a way of funding part of their winter travels to such culinary meccas as

Italy and France. I first became acquainted with the Villemaires when I noticed their fresh green shiso sitting all by itself at the market one Saturday. "Do you know what this is?" Mary asked me. "Oh yes, I do," I said, and we've been friends ever since. Bert and Mary grow the beautiful safflowers that I use on the Westside Bellini (page 95) and the Grapes of Roth (page 127). I also use their spearmint, Rainer and Bing cherries, pineapple guava blossoms, Thai basil, and lemon verbena. As lifelong foodies, the Villemaires' passion for beautiful produce is evident in everything they grow.

BIEKE AND BRIAN BURWELL

Some of the first friends I made in Healdsburg were Bieke and Brian Burwell, who eat at the Cyrus bar with an extended network of friends every Friday night. One member of this lively group, Mick

Kopetsky, is a professional gardener and landscape designer who designs and plants a lush, organic vegetable garden for the Burwells each spring. The garden produces far more than one family can use, so the Burwells offer the extra bounty to anyone who loves to cook and is willing to make the drive out to Dry Creek Valley. At the Cyrus bar, we use many of their basils, tomatoes, and peppers.

DRY CREEK PEACH AND PRODUCE

Brian Sullivan and Gayle Okumura Sullivan took over the Dry Creek peach orchard in the 1990s and made it 100 percent organic. Peaches are very difficult to grow organically, don't transport very well if ripened on the tree (the ones you buy in the grocery store generally aren't), and are subject to very low yields in certain years. This is no easy job, but the results are stellar. Dry Creek's white peaches make the most memorable Westside Bellinis (page 95), which we proudly feature at Cyrus for as long we can each summer.

HENRY AND COLLEEN FLORES

This local surgeon and his wife and family live on the north side of town, where they have a handful of pineapple guava bushes. Late in the fall, these plants produce small but intensely aromatic fruits that fall off the bush when ripe. The ones that are not eaten by their dog, Kiwi, are used in the Flores Margaritas (page 43).

KEN GRADEK

The Gradek family moved to their hundred-acre property in Dry Creek Valley in the 1950s, and five of the Gradek brothers and their families still live there today. I was introduced to Ken (see photo at left) through a mutual friend when I was looking for a new source of citrus. My eyes practically popped out of my head when I saw the Gradek's citrus knoll, where several kinds of oranges, lemons, and grapefruits flourish, along with pomelos the size of basketballs. The trees are decades old, and the Gradeks usually use very little of their huge bounty. As a bartender who loves fresh citrus cocktails, I felt like I'd found the mother lode. I trade Cyrus restaurant credit for access to Ken's citrus. The Gradeks also grow a dozen kinds of exceptional peaches and Asian pears that are so ethereal you'll shed a tear after each bite.

IRON HORSE VINEYARDS

The Sterling family's Iron Horse Vineyards released its first vintage in 1978 and has since become one of the most acclaimed producers of sparkling wine in the country. A trip to the winery is a must-do if you're visiting Sonoma. The panoramic views of Green Valley from the winery are unrivaled, the tasting room folks are as charming as can be, and the sparkling wines are some of the best you'll find. Barry Sterling, the patriarch of Iron Horse Vineyards, is not only a pioneer in the wine business but also a master gardener. His garden usually produces more tomatoes, chiles, and melons than the family can use, and they are kind enough to let us raid it a few times a year.

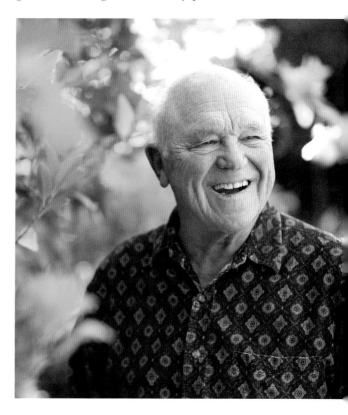

RAY LEWAND

The Camellia Inn is a small Victorian hotel in downtown Healdsburg owned by the Lewand family. Ray Lewand (see photo at right) has a ten-foot-tall Key lime tree that produces small fruit for about four months of the year, which we use in our Classic Margarita (page 41) and the Thai Monkey (page 33). Ray trades his limes for Hendrick's gin martinis and Chef Keane's billi-bi soup at the Cyrus bar.

LOVE FARMS

Ron and Bibiana Love live on a nine-acre organic farm on Healdsburg's Grove Street with their dog, Tiller. The farm is open to the public seven days a week during the nonrainy months, and the Loves also have a store just off the Healdsburg town square that sells produce, seedlings, and flowers. All of their goods are delivered in electric cars to local restaurants, and they don't sell to areas beyond the reach of these cars (which is not very far). The idea is to provide food for the community and its restaurants without using any fossil fuels.

Because the farm is only a half mile from Cyrus, I get to visit daily and pick whatever I need. The Loves are the first farmers I became friends with in Healdsburg, and having access to their farm is a big reason the cocktails at Cyrus look and taste so amazing.

BRUCE AND LIZ MCCONNELL

Although the McConnells own the Healdsburg Chevy dealership, growing perfect satsuma mandarins and Meyer lemons is their real passion. If frost is threatening his trees at four in the morning, Bruce (see photo at left) will bring out heaters to keep the air temperature just above freezing. Some of his trees are more than ten years old and produce 250 pounds of fruit each year. All of this hard work and dedication means the Cyrus bar gets perfect fruits for two to three months of the year. The McConnells insist on a trade-only policy, which means they can count on a couple of lavish dinners at the restaurant. Liz's heavenly Meyer lemon bars are also the official dessert of the afterlife.

THE NEWMANS

The chef at Cyrus, Douglas Keane, married Sonoma County local Lael Newman in 2006. Lael's father, Peter, has been growing grapes in Alexander Valley for decades. During harvest, Peter allocates a small amount of Merlot and Cabernet grapes for our use in the bar. We go out each fall and pick the grapes, then process most of them into juice and freeze the remaining small bunches for the Grapes of Roth (page 127).

PARTNERS IN GARLIC

Paul and Yael Bernier live on Canyon Road in Dry Creek Valley, where they grow many vegetables and, most famously, garlic. Paul was instrumental in getting the farmers' market certified in the late 1970s, and the couple was the original planters of the Dry Creek peach orchards (see page 138). Once a year, Yael picks all of the pomegranates from her trees and sells them in batches over the course of a few weeks at the markets. There is nothing more satisfying than chopping a whole pomegranate in half and pressing the crimson liquid out of its shell. This succulent juice is the basis for the PomIranian (page 123).

PRESTON VINEYARDS

At Preston Vineyards, located on West Dry Creek Road, you'll find much more than wine. Lou and Susan Preston are at the forefront of progressive farming, and the lengths they go to in order to make their farm both organic and sustainable are honorable. Their tractors even run on vegetable oil. I would encourage a visit if you happen to be in the area. You can buy several kinds of wine and port, olives and olive oil, eggs, bread, and seasonal vegetables. Many of their goods have found their way into the Cyrus bar program, including hot chiles and fresh horseradish, which the Prestons use to make their famous hot sauce.

RIDGEVIEW FARMS

Joel and Renee Kiff started Ridgeview Farms in 1978, one year before the Healdsburg Farmers' Market was founded. Originally, their property was used to raise animals as part of the local 4-H and Future Farmers of America programs, but over time they turned their focus to vegetables, fruit, and flowers. The Kiffs have persistently shown Healdsburg residents that producing food for your community and knowing the faces behind that food is very important. Joel and Renee and their daughter, Sarah (see photo at right), who specializes in flowers, sell at the two weekly farmers' markets. I buy

Ridgeview Farms olallieberries and marionberries, as well as the many varieties of apples I use in the Autumn Apple (page 115).

ROSE FAMILY FARM

It would be a serious understatement to say that Blanche Ienine-Cruz is passionate about what she does. Her obsession with producing the finest flowers, herbs, and vegetables is matched only by her deep knowledge of botany as a whole. Her small, organic Rose Family Farm is located in Graton in western Sonoma County. I'm fortunate to get many of Blanche's rare and unique goods at various times throughout the year.

SEBASTOPOL BERRY FARM

On the way to Iron Horse Vineyards on Ross Station Road, you pass Sebastopol Berry Farm, where during the brief berry season, the Vigil family sells blueberries, raspberries, marion-berries, olallieberries, and blackberries out of a small garage. They also sell at several farmers' markets in the area. If you ask nicely, they'll let you walk around the property to get a close-up look at a real blueberry bush, quite possibly the world's most perfect creation when it's bursting with berries in the summer.

DAN AND LAURA SOOY

The Sooys are good friends who live in a historic home on Matheson Street in Healdsburg. They have two ancient orange trees and a fifty-year-old Rangpur lime tree on their property that I harvest fruit from about four months of the year. I recently planted Kaffir lime, Bergamot orange, yuzu, Buddha's hand citron, and Australian finger lime trees on their property in hopes that they will be flourishing one hundred years from now.

MEET THE DISTILLERS

ALTHOUGH microdistilleries seem to be cropping up everywhere these days, Northern California has been home to some of the finest boutique distilleries for decades. Don't get me wrong, I'm a big fan of all types of spirits from around the world, but I like to use local spirits because many of them are unlike anything else on the market, and they work especially well with seasonal ingredients. Many of these distillers have become personal friends over the years, and being able to connect a human face with the brand means a great deal to me.

ANCHOR DISTILLERY

Besides single-handedly starting the microbrewery movement in the late 1960s by saving the Anchor Brewing Company from certain demise, Fritz Maytag (see photo at right) has also become an accomplished spirits maker. Everything Anchor produces gives recognition to local history: their steam beer has been made in much the same way for more than one hundred years, their rye whiskies are produced in the style of particular eras, and their gin is named for Junípero Serra, an eighteenth-century Franciscan

missionary in California. A visit to Anchor's Mariposa Street brewery and distillery in San Francisco's Potrero Hill neighborhood is a must-do for anyone passing through.

DISTILLERY NO. 209

The original Distillery No. 209 was located in St. Helena a hundred years ago, but when Leslie Rudd (of Dean and DeLuca, Rudd Winery, and Standard Beverages) attempted to reestablish it a few years back, the government wouldn't allow it. Instead, he set up a brand new distillery on Pier 50 in San Francisco. Master distiller Arnie Hillesland's (see photo top left) 209 gin, which incorporates only the finest botanicals, is excellent enjoyed on its own or in classic cocktails like the Negroni, or my take on it, the Rudd Negroni (page 63).

DOMAINE CHARBAY

Nestled about two thousand feet above St. Helena (southeast of Healdsburg in Napa Valley) is the "still on the hill," a local distillery called Domaine Charbay that is owned and operated by the Karakasevic family (see photo bottom left). Master distiller Miles Karakasevic and his wife, Susan, their daughter, Lara, and their son, Marko, represent the twelfth and thirteenth generations of distillers in this family. Marko's wife, Jenny, travels the country spreading the gospel of their handcrafted spirits.

In 1998, with the release of their Meyer lemon and blood orange products, Domaine Charbay became the first distillery to produce all-natural, fresh fruit–enhanced vodkas. Since then, they have produced about half a dozen other flavored vodkas, as well as pastis, barrel-strength whiskey, brandies, two kinds of pot-distilled rum, and great vintages of port and red wine. When these fine spirits are married with seasonal juices and fresh produce, truly fine cocktails are born.

GERMAIN-ROBIN

Hubert Germain-Robin's (see photo at right) family has been making brandies in Cognac, France, for generations, but it was only after arriving in Northern California in the late 1970s that he started making the unique brandies that he's known for now. Traditionally, Cognac is made from the high-yield Ugni Blanc grape varietal. In Mendocino County, Hubert began using Pinot Noir, Colombard, and other varietals. And while some of his brandies were blended, others needed nothing but a little local rainwater to cut them down to bottling strength. After thirty years of distilling in California, Hubert produced brandies that are consistently ranked higher than some of the world's oldest and rarest brands, many of which cost ten times more than his Germain-Robin XO.

Hubert has now left Germain-Robin, but he continues to live in Mendocino and works as an international consultant. Lucky for us, many of the brandies he made at Germain-Robin are still sleeping in barrels, continuing to mature and gain character.

ROTH VODKA

The Roth vodka label is owned by Ted and Nicole Simpkins of Lancaster Vineyards in Alexander Valley. Made entirely from California wine grapes, mostly French Colombard, Roth's subtle grapelike quality makes for an excellent martini, a tasty gimlet and, of course, a stunning Grapes of Roth (page 127).

SARTICIOUS SPIRITS

Sarticious Spirits, a small artisanal project located in Santa Cruz, California, is owned by Jeff Alexander and Mark Karakas. They make only gin—but what a gin it is. Juniper berries, orange, cardamom, ginger, fresh cilantro, and other secret ingredients combine to make a memorable product. Sarticious gin tastes particularly delicious in cocktails that incorporate fresh herbs or cucumbers, like the Sunny and Dry (page 83) and Frondsong (page 49).

ST. GEORGE SPIRITS

St. George Spirits is located near one of the old landing strips at the former Alameda Naval Station across the bay from San Francisco. In 1982, German-born Jörg Rupf began producing what are regarded as America's first authentic eau-de-vie using carefully selected pears, cherries, and raspberries. Since former Navy nuclear engineer and official "mad scientist" Lance Winters (see photo at left) joined the team in 1996, St. George Spirits has catapulted to the forefront of the microdistillery movement with the success of its Hangar One vodkas. Like the vodkas made at Domaine Charbay, they are enhanced with fresh, peak-of-season ingredients and made in very small batches. The distillery also produces single-malt whiskey, absinthe, and small cooperative ventures with other labels, including Qi tea-flavored liqueurs. What's next from St. George Spirits? You never know, but it never disappoints.

INDEX

A

Alexander, Jeff, 146
Anchor Distillery, 143–44
Apple Farm, 103
Apples
	Autumn Apple, 115–16
	Dehydrated Apple Chips, 116
April Shower, 47
Asian Pickling Liquid, 53
Autumn Apple, 115–16
Aviation, Mariposa, 62

B

Balsamic vinegar, 103
Beachfire Margarita, 42
Beau Regards, 76–77
Beau Regards Simple Syrup, 77
Bella Ruffina, 125
Bellini, Westside, 95–97
Bernier, Paul and Yael, 112, 136, 141
Blackberries
	Blackberry Lick, 89–90
Blood oranges
	Bleeding Orange, 26–27
	Winter Spice–Orange Sugar,
		26
Blueberries
	Beau Regards, 76–77

Bourbon
	Bourbon Infused with Vanilla
		and Citrus Peel, 72
	Frankfort Manhattan, 65
	Mint Julep, 85
	Pappy Old-Fashioned, 70
Brandy
	Autumn Apple, 115–16
	Mendo Sidecar, 67
	Painful Punch, 135
Burke, Andrea, 112
Burwell, Bieke and Brian, 137–38

C

Cabernet Grape Juice, 128
Cachaça
	Caipirinha, 37
Campari
	Rudd Negroni, 63
Candied Lemongrass, 132
Candied Meyer Lemon Peels, 19
Candied Rhubarb, 75–76
Celery root
	Celery Mary, 103–4
	Pickled Celery Root Threads,
		104
Cherries, 121
Chiffonade, 87

Chinese Five-Spice Syrup, 18
Chips
	Crispy Lotus Root Chips, 24
	Dehydrated Apple Chips, 116
	Dehydrated Peach Chips,
		96–97
Citrus fruits. *See also individual*
	fruits
	Hello Cello, 12
	juicing, 10–11, 60
	Pelo del Perro (Hair of the
		Dog), 15
Classic Margarita, 41
Coca-Cola
	Cuba Libre, 55
	Mexican, 60
Coconut milk
	Thai Boxer, 81
	Thai Monkey, 33
Cointreau
	Beachfire Margarita, 42
	Classic Margarita, 41
	Flores Margarita, 43
	Mendo Sidecar, 67
Cranberry juice, 60
Creole Watermelon, 107–8
Crispy Lotus Root Chips, 24
Cuba Libre, 55

Cucumbers
    Pimm's Cup, 109
    Preserved Cucumber, 84
    Sunny and Dry, 83–84
D
Daikon
    Gin Kimchi, 51
    Pickled Daikon, 54
Dark and Stormy, 59
Dehydrated Apple Chips, 116
Dehydrated Peach Chips, 96–97
Dionysos, Marco, 1
Distillers, 143–46
Distillery No. 209, 144
Domaine Charbay, 144–45
Dry Creek Peach and Produce,
        95, 138
Dry Soda, 60
E, F
Egg whites, foams from, 30
Essential oils, syrups infused
        with, 21
Fennel
    Frondsong, 49
    Pickled Fennel, 52–53
Fever-Tree, 57, 60
Five-Spice Marinated Mandarin
        Orange Segments, 19
Flores, Henry and Colleen, 138
Flores Margarita, 43
Flowers, edible, 129
Foams, 28–30
Frankfort Manhattan, 65
Fraser River Sour, 92–93
Frondsong, 49
Fruits. *See also individual fruits*
    dehydrating, 113
    juicing, 10–11, 60
G
Germain-Robin, Hubert, 145
Gin, 46
    April Shower, 47
    Frondsong, 49

Gin and Tonic, 57
Gin Kimchi, 51
The Last Word, 71
Mariposa Aviation, 62
Rudd Negroni, 63
Sunny and Dry, 83–84
Ginger
    Ginger-Shisho Syrup, 51
    Ginger Simple Syrup, 116
    Gin Kimchi, 51
    Pickled Ginger, 54
Ginger beer, 60, 80
    Dark and Stormy, 59
    Gin Kimchi, 51
    Irian Jaya, 131–32
    Thai Boxer, 81
    Thai Monkey, 33
Glasses, 6–7
Gradek, Ken, 138–39
Grapes. *See also* Verjuice; Wine
    Cabernet Grape Juice, 128
    Grapes of Roth, 127–28
Green Chartreuse
    Frondsong, 49
    The Last Word, 71
    Thai Monkey, 33
H
Handy Sazerac, 69
Hanna, David, 135
Healdsburg Farmers' Market,
        3, 136–42
Heirloom Tomato Juice, 100
Heirloom Tomato Water, 101
Hello Cello, 12
Herbs, 87
Hillesland, Arnie, 144
Hot Buttered Rum, 119–20
Hot Indian Date, 35–36
Hot Tamarind Syrup, 36
Huckleberries
    Huck Yu, 91
Hyssop Simple Syrup, 90

I, J, K
Ice, 5, 58
Ienine-Cruz, Blanche, 142
Irian Jaya, 131–32
Iron Horse Vineyards, 139
Juicing, 10–11, 60
Karakas, Mark, 146
Karakasevic family, 144
Keane, Douglas, 3, 140
Kiff, Joel and Renee, 89, 136, 141–42
Kopetsky, Mick, 137
L
Lancaster Vineyards, 127
The Last Word, 71
La Bonne Terre, 137
Lemongrass
    Candied Lemongrass, 132
    Irian Jaya, 131–32
    Lemongrass Lemonade, 133
Lemons. *See also* Meyer lemons
    April Shower, 47
    Blackberry Lick, 89–90
    Fraser River Sour, 92–93
    Frondsong, 49
    Gin Kimchi, 51
    Lemongrass Lemonade, 133
    Mariposa Aviation, 62
    Mendo Sidecar, 67
    Pimm's Cup, 109
    Plum Dandy, 99
    Rhubarbarella, 75–76
    Sunny and Dry, 83–84
Lewand, Ray, 139
Limes
    Beachfire Margarita, 42
    Caipirinha, 37
    Classic Margarita, 41
    Flores Margarita, 43
    Irian Jaya, 131–32
    The Last Word, 71
    Mojito, 86
    Thai Boxer, 81
    Thai Monkey, 33

Limoncello
    Hello Cello, 12
    Huck Yu, 91
Lotus root
    Crispy Lotus Root Chips, 24
    Lotus Potion, 23–24
Love, Ron and Bibiana, 4, 139–40
Love Farms, 4, 139–40
M
Mandarin oranges
    Five-Spice Marinated Mandarin
        Orange Segments, 19
    Waverly Place Echo, 17–19
Manhattan, Frankfort, 65
Margaritas
    Beachfire Margarita, 42
    Classic Margarita, 41
    Flores Margarita, 43
Marionberries
    Blackberry Lick, 89–90
Mariposa Aviation, 62
Maytag, Fritz, 143
McConnell, Bruce and Liz, 17, 140
Mendo Sidecar, 67
Mescal
    Beachfire Margarita, 42
Meyer lemons
    Bleeding Orange, 26–27
    Candied Meyer Lemon Peels, 19
    Lotus Potion, 23–24
    Meyer Beautiful (My, You're
        Beautiful), 13
    Thai Monkey, 33
    Waverly Place Echo, 17–19
Mint
    Mint Julep, 85
    Mint Simple Syrup, 84
    Mojito, 86
Mixers, 60–61
Mojito, 86
Morgan, Jack, 80
Muddling, 87

N, O
Nana Mae's Organics, 61
Navarro Vineyards, 61
Negroni, Rudd, 63
Newman family, 127, 140
Olallieberries
    Blackberry Lick, 89–90
Old-Fashioned, Pappy, 70
Onions
    April Shower, 47
    Pickled Pearl Onions, 53
Oranges. See also Blood oranges
    Lotus Potion, 23–24
    Painful Punch, 135
P
Painful Punch, 135
Palms, heart of
    Hot Indian Date, 35–36
    Pickled Hearts of Palm, 36
Pappy Old-Fashioned, 70
Partners in Garlic, 141
Peaches
    Dehydrated Peach Chips,
        96–97
    Westside Bellini, 95–97
    White Peach Puree, 96
Pelo del Perro (Hair of the Dog), 15
Peppers
    Irian Jaya, 131–32
    Pickled Nardello Peppers, 132
Peterson, Tom, 136
Peyton, Nick, 3
Pickles
    Pickled Celery Root Threads,
        104
    Pickled Daikon, 54
    Pickled Fennel, 52–53
    Pickled Ginger, 54
    Pickled Hearts of Palm, 36
    Pickled Nardello Peppers, 132
    Pickled Pearl Onions, 53

Pickling liquids
    Asian Pickling Liquid, 53
    Ultimate Pickling Liquid, 52
Pimm's Cup, 109
Pineapple
    Painful Punch, 135
Pineapple guavas
    Flores Margarita, 43
Pinel, Andre, 112
Plum Dandy, 99
Pomegranates
    Pomiranian, 123–24
Preserved Cucumber, 84
Preston, Lou and Susan, 112, 141
Preston Vineyards, 141
Punch, Painful, 135
Purple Berry Syrup, 90
R
Rangpur limes
    Hot Indian Date, 35–36
Raspberries
    Fraser River Sour, 92–93
    Raspberry–Lemon Verbena
        Syrup, 93
Rhubarb
    Candied Rhubarb, 75–76
    Rhubarbarella, 75–76
Ridgeview Farms, 89, 141–42
Rims, salted and sugared, 38–39
Rose Family Farm, 142
Roth Vodka, 145–46
Rudd, Leslie, 144
Rudd Negroni, 63
Rum
    Cuba Libre, 55
    Dark and Stormy, 59
    Fraser River Sour, 92–93
    Hot Buttered Rum, 119–20
    Hot Indian Date, 35–36
    Mojito, 86
    Painful Punch, 135
    Thai Boxer, 81

Rupf, Jörg, 146
Rye whiskey
    Handy Sazerac, 69
S
St. George Spirits, 92, 146
Salt
    on rims, 38–39
    types of, 38
Sarticious Spirits, 146
Sazerac, Handy, 69
Sebastopol Berry Farm, 89, 142
Seltzer Sisters, 61
Sidecar, Mendo, 67
Simpkins, Ted and Nicole, 127, 145
Simple syrup. *See* Syrups
Sodas, 60–61
Sonoma Sparkler, 61
Sooy, Dan and Laura, 23, 142
Spiced Pomegranate Juice, 124
Spices
    on rims, 39
    syrups infused with, 20–21
    toasting, 20–21
    Winter Spice–Orange Sugar,
        26
    Winter Spice Syrup, 27
Staining, 73
Sterling, Barry, 139
Sugar
    on rims, 38–39
    types of, 38
    Winter Spice–Orange Sugar,
        26
Sullivan, Brian and Gayle
        Okumura, 95, 138
Sunny and Dry, 83–84
Sweet and sour mix, 61
Syrups
    Beau Regards Simple Syrup, 77
    Chinese Five-Spice Syrup, 18
    Ginger-Shisho Syrup, 51

Ginger Simple Syrup, 116
Hot Tamarind Syrup, 36
Huckleberry Syrup, 91
Hyssop Simple Syrup, 90
infusing, with essential oils, 21
infusing, with spices, 20–21
Mint Simple Syrup, 84
Purple Berry Syrup, 90
Raspberry–Lemon Verbena
    Syrup, 93
Rhubarbarella Syrup, 75–76
simple, 20
Winter Spice Syrup, 27

T
Tamarind
    Hot Indian Date, 35–36
Tequila
    Beachfire Margarita, 42
    Classic Margarita, 41
    Flores Margarita, 43
    Pelo del Perro (Hair of the
        Dog), 15
Thai Boxer, 81
Thai Monkey, 33
Tomatoes
    Celery Mary, 103–4
    Heirloom Tomato Juice, 100
    Heirloom Tomato Water, 101
    The Upstairs Neighbor, 105
U, V
Ultimate Pickling Liquid, 52
The Upstairs Neighbor, 105
Verjuice, 90
    April Shower, 47
    Grapes of Roth, 127–28
    Huck Yu, 91
Vermouth
    Bella Ruffina, 125
    Frankfort Manhattan, 65
    Rudd Negroni, 63
Vigil family, 142

Villemaire, Bert and Mary, 137
Vodka, 80
    Beau Regards, 76–77
    Blackberry Lick, 89–90
    Bleeding Orange, 26–27
    Celery Mary, 103–4
    Creole Watermelon, 107–8
    Fraser River Sour, 92–93
    Grapes of Roth, 127–28
    Hello Cello, 12
    Huck Yu, 91
    Irian Jaya, 131–32
    Lotus Potion, 23–24
    Meyer Beautiful (My, You're
        Beautiful), 13
    Pelo del Perro (Hair of the
        Dog), 15
    Plum Dandy, 99
    Pomiranian, 123–24
    Rhubarbarella, 75–76
    Thai Monkey, 33
    The Upstairs Neighbor, 105
    Waverly Place Echo, 17–19
W
Watermelon
    Creole Watermelon, 107–8
    Watermelon Juice, 108
Waverly Place Echo, 17–19
Westside Bellini, 95–97
Whiskey. *See* Bourbon; Rye whiskey
White Peach Puree, 96
Wine
    Bella Ruffina, 125
    Huck Yu, 91
    Painful Punch, 135
    Plum Dandy, 99
    Westside Bellini, 95–97
Winters, Lance, 92, 146
Winter Spice–Orange Sugar, 26
Winter Spice Syrup, 27